Supervising Today

**Wiley Series
in Training
and Development**

Editor: Charles T. Peers, Jr.

Succession Planning: Key to Corporate Excellence
by Arthur X. Deegan, II

Supervising Technical and Professional People
by Martin M. Broadwell and Ruth Seizmore House

Supervising Today: A Guide for Positive Leadership,
Second Edition
by Martin M. Broadwell

Moving Up to Supervision, Second Edition
by Martin M. Broadwell

tc Supervising Today ⌐

A GUIDE FOR
POSITIVE LEADERSHIP

SECOND EDITION

Martin M. Broadwell
General Manager, Center for Management Services, Inc.

Cartoons by Johnny Sajem

A Wiley-Interscience Publication

JOHN WILEY & SONS
New York / Chichester / Brisbane / Toronto / Singapore

Library of Congress Cataloging in Publication Data:

Broadwell, Martin M.
  Supervising today.

  (Wiley series in training and development)
  "A Wiley-Interscience publication."
  Includes index.
  1. Supervision of employees. I. Title. II. Series.
HF5549.B857   1986   658.3'02   85-29576
ISBN 0-471-83674-5

Printed in the United States of America

10 9 8 7 6 5 4 3 2 1

To Tim

He came from this generation,
made it to the top,
learned a lot along the way
and taught me much of what's here!

Preface

When *Supervising Today* first came out, it was the first book that was aimed at assisting "old-line" supervisors in understanding the new workforce. For the supervisors, who had grown up in the Great Depression or during the years of World War II, there were conflicts in life style, relationships, attitudes toward life, work, and the world in general, and the commonly perceived view held by the new workforce that a job was just that—only a job. Neither the supervisors nor the subordinates were even close to being able to understand the value systems of the other, and the gap contributed to some miserable times at the workplace. The first edition of *Supervising Today* attempted to explain not only the evolution of the new value systems, but how to supervise where such values were held by subordinates.

The "new workforce" is no longer so new. Its value systems still exist and are held by those who are just coming into the workplace. Indeed, many of the values have permeated even the older workforce, because the same conditions exist now as have existed since this older group came into the establishment's domain of work in the 1960s.

The same pressures are here for the supervisors, the same attitudes exist, and the same external and internal influences of profit needs, safety, equal employment, and governmental regulations are present. Another factor has been added: Many of the "new workforce" are now coming into the supervisory ranks, confounding the problem even further.

This book was originally published with limited distribution by a publisher less known in the human resources field, and hence has had limited publicity. However, it has been received well by those who have used it. The users have urged it be more widely distributed and brought up to date. This second edition, published by a well-known and highly respected publisher, is designed to fulfill those requests. Three major additions appear in this edition:

1. Study and discussion questions have been added at the end of each chapter to facilitate its use as a textbook in supervisory training classes.

2. The new Chapter 9, Delegation, is a lengthy examination of how important the skill of delegation is when dealing with the new workforce. When used correctly, delegation has proven to be a very useful tool in motivating this group.

3. Chapter 13, Supervising Tomorrow, examines the new workforce and shows where it appears to be going, both as the members of this group become supervisors and as they find themselves competing with their own massive numbers in a narrow age group.

This is not intended to be a psychology book or a social science text. There is no attempt to prove malice, fault, condemnation, or commendation for any one group of people. This second edition explores the continuing mysteries of how to survive with the conditions as they are. The solutions are still there, updated. It is the author's hope that the reading will be fun and the solutions usable!

MARTIN M. BROADWELL

Decatur, Georgia
April 1986

Preface to the First Edition

There is a conflict in our thinking as to whether people change. There seems to be no doubt that people are different today in their thinking, in their attitudes toward work and the boss, and in their value systems as a whole. But are people really different in their basic nature?

This book deals with this question from the standpoint of the supervisor, who has the job of getting the work out with the employees available. It is not a book about change, but a book that shows the supervisor that we can count on some things about people being the same all the time. It gives guides for dealing with people and with the job of supervision in a positive way rather than from the standpoint that the supervisor's entire job is worrying about problems. PMA, or positive mental attitude, is a key to success; and this book aims to give supervisors enough skills and background information to help develop this important PMA.

It isn't enough to tell people about supervision. They need some guidelines and some steps to follow to help them supervise well. This book is straightforward; it proposes to tell a supervisor how to survive and succeed in the present work world. The workforce comprises a new generation of workers who differ from the older workers in both values and ideals. Taken as a whole, they are better educated and more ambitious in many ways than any older generation. And they don't know the meaning of "You can't do it this way." The effective supervisor can use this new thinking process in a positive way and create excitement about the job from the viewpoint of both the supervisor and the subordinate.

There are many good books on supervision. This one is different only in that it is new enough to take the old standbys—Maslow, Herzberg, and all the rest—and put new looks to them in light of what has been learned about the present generation. It admits that problems exist and that the supervisor cannot solve them all. It goes beyond theory to some basic answers to the question, "What do I do when the workers show up?" If it is successful, it will be because the readers go beyond the theory and the reasons why there are problems and develop the positive mental attitude that says, "Hey, maybe I *can* be a good supervisor!"

MARTIN M. BROADWELL

Decatur, Georgia
1979

Acknowledgments

Many people have contributed to this book. Even under-standing the hazards of starting to mention names, I want to express my thanks to those training people who have made first-hand contact with hundreds of old-time, first-line supervisors possible for me during training sessions. This is particularly true of Bill Fiffick, Joel Ramich, Bob Rock, and Irv Scherman. Most especially, though, I must mention Margie Garrett, whose efforts at taking pages out of my typewriter and with careful editing, transforming them into readable, meaningful copy are gratefully ac-knowledged.

M. M. B.

Prologue

Before reading any book, one ought to think about why one is reading it. This book isn't the answer to all of anyone's problems, but it will answer a few problems for some people. It deals with basic supervision, but many books do that. It also deals with the younger workforce, and fewer books do that. It puts the two things together, and even fewer books try to do that. If you have problems with the younger generation, you aren't unique. If you have problems supervising people of any age, you aren't unique either; most people do, whether they admit it or not. You will not solve all your problems by reading this book, but you will find some reasons why you have some problems, and that will help a lot. You'll discover that you can do some things to make supervision easier and more satisfying. There's nothing in this book that isn't working for somebody with problems just like yours in situations just like yours. So, take heart; they may even work for you. At least it's worth a try.

Contents

PART FOUR   POSITIVE SUPERVISION

part one

Introduction

Chapter one

The Nature of Today's Working People

To the old-line, experienced supervisor who joined the organization thirty to forty years ago, it is no surprise that the work force has changed from what it was a generation ago. However, the supervisor who came into the work ranks just a few years ago may wonder if much of a change has taken place. It is between these two groups that the well-known generation gap shows up. There has, indeed, been a change in working people—a change so drastic that we've never before seen the likes of it in the history of our country. Admittedly, there have always been changes from one generation to the next when the children of any given work force follow their parents into the labor market. Although every supervisor looks at the new employee and thinks, "There's no way I can get the job done with *this* kind of help!", the change we're talking about has roots in events that took place over a period of years. While the outcome could have been predicted, little could have been done to change it.

What is the conflict? Why does it exist? Is there a chance that the present workers aren't different, but just that the older generation is seeing them in a different light? Is there a solution to the problem? These questions are being asked by workers, supervisors, and employment sections of the organizations as well as by social scientists and industrial psychologists. Fortunately, there are some real answers to some very real problems. The situation isn't hopeless, but today's experienced supervisors are going to have to understand some things if they hope to be successful. Those new supervisors mentioned earlier also must find out some things to be able to relate to both the experienced supervisors and working people.

The differences in working people are reflected in many ways. Most noticeably, there is a difference between the value system of the present-day worker and that of the worker who was hired in the two decades following World War II. Changes have occurred in the way the worker looks at the organization, the bosses, the management, the "establishment," and the work itself. These differences—stemming from the different value systems—also show up in personal lives. These workers hold a quite different view of the community and their place in it, their families, marriage, and morality.

The solution lies not just in understanding where the workers got their attitudes and values, but in learning how to modify our *traditional* approaches to people and supervising people. This means that there is a problem in adjusting because the change must come within the group that is the least prone to make changes—the older, established supervisors. No unkindness is intended here when we say that they are simply set in their ways and see no reason to make any changes. And if changes are going to be made, they would prefer to see their new subordinates make them, for they certainly feel that their own value system is far superior to the new generation's. This is the impasse that must be dealt with if any understanding is to be reached. The solution lies not in changing the value system of either the new workers or the experienced supervisors but in understanding the younger workers and taking a supervisory approach that will provide the results we want from them.

THE "ESTABLISHMENT"

To understand the people who have been coming into the labor market since the early seventies, it is necessary first to see how the older supervisors came to get their value system. They make up the "older" generation that the present generation labeled as the "establishment." When the new generation coined the phrase "Don't trust anyone over thirty," they were talking about people like these experienced supervisors, who thought a lot alike, had much in common, and weren't too different from their own parents in their thinking and beliefs. For the most part, they had little conflict with their supervision when they came on board; if anything was different, they may have worked a little harder because they were glad to have jobs. They represented the epitome of the "American work ethic."

These experienced supervisors had lived through a major depression and a world war. They knew what it was like to go without and not to be able to have everything their way. Their home life was fairly stable, and because they had no television, most of their activities centered around the family. In many ways, they were reasonably sheltered and naive when they went to work. Because they had been through a depression, money was important to them, and they measured success in terms of the job they had, the money they made, and how much money they could *save.* When they got jobs, they were appreciative of and loyal to the organization. They did not think the organization was always right, but it had given them jobs and hence could tell them what to do. Even though they might not like their bosses, they rarely doubted that the bosses were in full control of the work situation.

Job changing occasionally took place, but it was not an everyday occurrence to see somebody move from one company or organization to another. Organizations tended to think that anyone who had worked for more than one other organization was unstable, and they were wary of hiring that person. When today's supervisors were new employees, they usually considered things like security, benefits, and certainly the pension or retirement plans. In the fifties and early sixties, the organizations recruiting on college campuses had trouble hiring top-notch people unless they offered healthy *benefits programs* that included attractive retirement plans.

Perhaps nothing marks these experienced supervisors more than their feelings about money, promotion, and their niche in the organization. Because they knew what it was like not to have money, they were very conscious of it, worrying about raises and saving their earnings. They were interested in stock-purchase plans and payroll savings, and often they were still buying government bonds through payroll deductions. Most could remember their first bicycle, their first suit, and their first automobile—if they had one. Many could point to these things and say that they had worked to get them, saving their money over a long period. They understood that things didn't come easily, and they were even accustomed to realizing that they *couldn't* have some things they wanted. As far as promotion was concerned, they realized that it came to those who worked and waited. They were willing to work on the same job, even a dull job that they learned in a reasonably short time, until a promotion came along. They celebrated a

raise or a promotion by taking their family out to dinner—
something they didn't do very often. When they were out
with others who worked at a different place, they could be
heard boasting about their own organization. They resented anyone finding fault with it and would defend it
without shame. Their children showed the same loyalty at
school and on the playground.

The vast majority of the people of this generation had
mothers who worked very hard at home, canning, washing,
and cooking. Their families had conveniences, but in
many cases these only added more work. Washing machines could take bigger loads, but the clothes had to be
ironed. Pressure cookers were more convenient, but they
made it possible to go out and buy things by the bushel, if
there was no home garden. The mothers of these older supervisors stayed at home, and in many cases there were so
few children in the neighborhood that mothers even provided part of the "play force," learning to play baseball
and catch.

It is not surprising that the people who made up the supervisory ranks in the 1950s thought alike and had about
the same value system their parents did. They spent much
time with their parents. They stayed at home longer and
started to school later, since there were few nursery
schools and kindergartens. Not as many went to college,
especially away to college. There wasn't much interference at meals, and parents and children spent the evening
mealtime together. Though they might have kept the radio
on, television wasn't around, and they didn't know how to
pull TV dinners out of the freezer, pop them into the micro-
wave oven, and put them on a TV tray so everyone could
rush to watch television instead of talking during the meal.
While the children who became our older supervisors
didn't always agree with their parents, at least they learned
to *know* their parents and listen to them. Because of this,

they developed many of the same value systems their parents had. These value systems followed them into the work place.

A NEW GENERATION

When the war was over in 1945, things had already started to change. The "boys" had left home and "seen the world." People became more mobile. GIs came home with money or some access to it. If they went to college, the government paid their tuition and also paid them a monthly income. Many of these "boys" went to college and became the first in their families to get degrees. Home life became different, too. Mothers had taken jobs in factories, and for the first time many families had more money than they needed for food. During the war, with the depression over, many people had made a great deal of money. With nothing to spend it on and with their penchant for saving, these people had boosted the war effort by buying war bonds. When rationing ended, they had the money to buy things and go places. Starting in the late forties, people were married and babies were born at a greater rate than ever before in the history of this country. It was these babies that began to make up the "New Generation."

The children who grew up immediately after the war were the largest group of children under ten years old in the country's history. With better than forty percent of the total population under fifteen years old at one time, the whole country seemed to turn all its attention to this age group. Coincident with their births came the birth of another phenomenon that made itself felt in American life from the day it came on the market: television. Starting in the late 1940s, television grew up with this new generation.

It helped set values in at least two ways. First, both children and parents spent their time glued to the screens, which at first had little more than test patterns, but which soon became a powerhouse of influence. Programmers soon became aware of the number of children in the audience, and the advertisers were right with them. Both programs and commercials constantly appealed to the children viewers. Even if this had not been so, the fact that children spent so much time watching television meant that in their formative years their value system was built by this medium. Second, the time that the children spent watching television was time that families formerly spent in *conversation.* TV dinners on TV tables replaced the dinner table and the values that came from mealtime togetherness. Gradually there arose a gap in communications. There just wasn't much talking going on, and parents and children never really gained much experience in speaking to each other. The absence of such conversation led to misunderstandings that often were not really corrected.

Oddly enough, at a time when there were more children than ever before, nearly the entire country was pampering the children more than ever before. Post-war affluence could provide for their every need (or *want*), and television taught them about plenty of things to need and want. Basically, parents were telling their children, "I want you to have it better than I did." "Better" almost always was interpreted as having more material things; being allowed to do more, see more, and go more; and having fewer restrictions. All the institutions that could offer services to children did so with great approval by all concerned. More schools were built because children were starting to crowd the existing classrooms. Nursery schools and kindergartens sprang up, often because the mothers were working and the children needed to be away from home

earlier than ever before. Communities offered other services, too, such as clubs and organizations. Little leagues,
scout troops, Campfire Girls, and combinations of all these
things grew in number and influence. They, too, had their
part in influencng the children, but for the most part they
just *provided places for children to be together.* The children's value system weren't necessarily being set by the
group leaders, but rather by the many other children they
spent their time with. Church groups offered a hand, too.
Many religious organizations opened their doors as *community centers,* where less religion and more recreation
became the way of life. "Anything for the children" was the
constant cry, while the doomsayers warned us that we
were "losing our children." The truth was, however, that we
didn't lose them: we just didn't know them when they grew
up.

THE VALUE SYSTEM

The end product of all this doting on children—giving
them everything their parents never had—was a generation of people who had never known what it was like really
to *want something* material and not get it. They were given
much but never had to give much in return. They were better educated than any age group had ever been. As a result of both their education and their television watching,
they were more aware of what was going on in the world.
They had much confidence in themselves but little confidence in the "establishment" that had tried so hard to
make them independent. They had become even more independent than their parents had imagined they could be.
They felt no need to compete with adults, only with themselves. Often the competition was rigged so that every-

body got to play, and maybe win, because that was a rule of the organized activities in which they participated. With all the group experience that they had acquired, in certain ways they were better able to think and act on their own than their parents had been. (We'll see later, however, that this wasn't true in the work world.)

The product of this child-oriented society was a generation that in most cases received immediate gratification. Whatever they wanted, they got when they wanted it, not after waiting or saving money. Although not on purpose, they were trained to expect to receive what they felt they needed at the time they discovered the need. "Everybody else is doing it" or "everybody else has it" were reasons enough to get it right then. Almost overnight they made drastic changes in college life and curricula. If they thought that cafeteria workers weren't making enough money, they simply sat down in front of the cafeteria until changes were made. If they saw no reason for certain requirements in the catalog, the catalogs were changed *that semester.*

This isn't to say that everything the new generation did was wrong; not every change they suggested was incorrect. Their experiences and education had given them an insight into reasons for things; if they didn't see the reason, they asked, "Why?" Often there was no reason other than that things had always been done this way. Although the young saw that many of the rules, policies, and requirements had been formulated for times and situations that were now outdated, in many cases they failed to recognize the experience and wisdom that had gone into getting things the way they were. They had learned to spot hypocrisy, and thus they quickly detected vast conflicts between claims of freedom and the social injustices they saw around them. They saw contrasts between the search for happiness and the misery of materialism. They had had time to "smell the roses," but they saw the pollution in the streams and forests. They saw faults that their parents knew were present but had either learned to live with or to ignore. They saw flaws in big business and in government. Although they generally had plenty, they never had to fight for a living in the work world. Consequently, they saw a need for everyone to get a share of the wealth. They had "learned" that big business was not really interested in anything constructive. With no previous contact with the traditional working environment, they had learned from the television medium and from their instructors and their peers; few of these influences did much to build confidence in the business climate. Essentially, the new generation was brought up to find something or someone to blame, and business, government, and schools were the most readily available and visible targets. In some cases, the parents got the blame because "they just didn't understand." All their criticisms made a lot of sense to them, but, as could have been predicted, they finally came face to face with the reality of many things: *They came into the work world.*

CONFLICT WITH THE WORK PLACE

We have seen that the supervisors in the work place had standards or systems of values that were pretty stable and very similar to those of their parents and supervisors before them. They had fairly uniform attitudes toward the organization, their bosses, and work itself. Their values and their priorities were in harmony with the organization, and for the most part they were loyal to the organization and its goals. *They were almost totally unprepared for the new generation who came to work for them.* Considering that

"A 2-day suspension? Could you make it Wednesday and Thursday? I'm scheduled off Friday through Sunday."

the new generation was in many ways even less prepared to go to work for them, conflict was inevitable. Such a conflict was predictable, but few predicted it. Most of the insight into the problem has actually come with hindsight.

An added problem for the new workers was that for the first time in their lives, they found themselves in the *minority*. They came into a place that was not designed to meet their needs and found themselves working for a person and an organization that did not exist because there were so many young people. Although this had been true as they progressed from nurseries and kindergartens through clubs, youth groups, and recreation halls to schools and colleges that had undergone massive expansions just for them, the places where they now found themselves had *not* been created for them. Young workers who came from backgrounds where everyone listened to them and made changes based on their wants, desires, and ideas, now found themselves working in places that frequently didn't even provide them with a means of *being heard,* much less listened to. If action was taken, it was taken as a result of suggestions from the older, experienced workers or supervisors. Frequently, even these suggestions were ignored while top management formulated all policies. To say that this frustrated new employees is an understatement. They found that they were expected to be loyal, to perform without reasoning, and to do the job they were to do without question, and that they were *not* expected to contribute anything constructive to the organization. Combined with their value system, all this gave loyalty to the organization a low priority with these new workers. Furthermore, little that was done for them and about them was conducive to building any loyalty. They were in the work place, but it was a strange and hostile place, partly because of their attitudes and partly because of the system in which they were expected to perform. Though it wasn't to their liking, they had to find out the hard way that they weren't going to change it much. At the same time, the organization that had hired them, and especially the old-line supervisors who were supervising them, didn't find the new employees to their particular liking. They, too, were to learn the hard way that this new generation wasn't about to be remolded. Many of the older supervisors saw the solution simply as having these new workers either staighten up or get out. Not many "straightened up," and when the others got out, their replacements came from the same mold.

NEITHER GOOD NOR BAD

Again, this isn't meant to imply that either group is right or wrong, good or bad. It's simply a case of vast differences in value systems. Each may see the other as right or wrong, good or bad, but that's only the value system at work. For example, one might say it's impolite to put elbows on the table, whereas another may see nothing wrong with it. In a situation like this, which has no moral or ethical basis, logic or argument won't settle the matter. One has a value system that makes elbows on the table hideous beyond words; the other has a value system that finds it a most comfortable way to eat. Based entirely on rearing or what they were told was right or wrong, each sees his or her way as *right*. If we can keep this in mind, it will help us understand not only the problem but also the solution when it is presented.

CONCLUSION

Where does all this leave us? To recap, we find ourselves faced with both a current and an oncoming generation of workers who have a value system quite different from that of the existing supervisors who have the responsibility for getting work from them. Their attitudes on *vital issues* are so different that there seems to be no common ground. At the same time, neither group is likely to change much, and certainly neither is in a position to develop an entirely new value system, since its basis is in early childhood and takes years to form.

Some have said that identifying the problem is half the battle, but such may not be the case here. If the younger people have attitudes that conflict with the organization's, if they aren't going to change them, if their replacements look just like them, and if the organization is set in its ways, the solution is surely more than "half-way away." There is a solution, though, and we'll try to find it in the chapters ahead. To this extent, this becomes a sort of a mystery book, but looking at the last chapter won't help because the solution is complex, and finding it will take careful plotting and analysis. Clue: Fortunately, we know a lot about *people in general.* We know some things about human nature, and human nature doesn't change. It is from these principles that we can draw our solution. While we can't do the same old things and get the results we want, we can look at the same attributes of human behavior and apply the rules in different ways.

DISCUSSION QUESTIONS

1. Discuss the value systems of both the new generation workers and those who have been in the work force for thirty or forty years.

2. What are some of the things that have contributed to the different value systems?

3. List some problems that have arisen as a result of the different attitudes and values from the perspective of the new generation, of the "establishment," and discuss the resulting changes in the role of the supervisor.

4. We have seen that part of the solution to the problem lies in recognizing and understanding the conflicting value systems. Where do we go from here?

Chapter two

The Changing Role
of the Supervisor

In Chapter 1 we talked about changing worker attitudes and the causes for this change. It is important that we recognize not only that most of the new workers have new attitudes, but also that one result is an extremely wide *mismatch* between the attitudes of the newer workers and the traditional attitudes of the supervisors. The plot thickens, though, when we realize that the workers aren't the only elements of organizations that are changing, but that the organizations themselves are undergoing some real changes, even though they may be less drastic and obvious.

Admittedly, organizations have changed to try to cope better with the workers' changing value systems, but in many ways other influences are more potent and affect the organizations much more dramatically. The political and social changes brought about by new societal viewpoints and by pressures from the media are having an impact on almost all phases of the business and industrial world. As we'll see in this chapter, competition has changed, but perhaps the most significant force on all levels of the organization is the outside force of government regulations. Within fewer than two decades, new laws and regulations have affected every function and every phase of the business world. An organization can make virtually no moves without considering a law violation, a potential investigation, and a legal question having to do with some local, state, or federal enforcement agency. Without arguing the merits of such regulations or delving into why they have become necessary, we can simply say that they are there and will be there for a long time; if the job gets done, it will get done by taking these regulations into consideration.

Another factor that has produced the subtle changes in the supervisor's role is that in the last couple of decades we've discovered a lot more about people and how to supervise them. This doesn't mean that we've come all the way or that we didn't know very much twenty years ago; but, as with any kind of science or skill, we find out more as time goes by and research goes on. There has not been a time in the last half-century that we haven't been studying about people in the supervisor-subordinate relationship. We simply know more now than we used to. Although we are not even close to practicing all we know or to figuring out how to apply all we've learned, at least we're farther along than we were. It is not true that we have "gone full cycle," as some would tell us. We do go back to some of the things we used to practice, but as often as not they are either things we had forgotten to do or things we go back to in ignorance, not knowing that they didn't work when we tried them in the past. Newly appointed, untrained supervisors are the ones most likely to make these errors. This book will point out some of the things learned over the years and how to apply them to supervision. In this chapter we'll look at why the supervisor's role has changed and what effect the changes have had on the way we supervise.

CHANGING ORGANIZATIONS

As we have already seen, both employees and organizations have changed. We'll see later that the organizations have modified their traditional behavior in many different ways for many reasons, but here let's just note that the jobs within the organizations have also changed, resulting in changes in the organizations themselves. Overall, organizations have diversified; they now do more different things than they used to. New technologies, increased competition, mergers, and changes in corporate and organizational structures have produced certain changes in jobs. The irony is that, while the organizations are doing more things than they used to, the individual employees are frequently doing *fewer different things* than ever before.

Over the past several years, we have come into the true age of specialization. When a new technology, such as computer technology, is introduced, a wave of new, highly specialized jobs appears. There is little cross-training; even though people work in the same department, for the most part they cannot interchange their jobs. Gone are the days of the across-the-board expert. Gone, too, are the simple job descriptions that used to characterize the generalist. Job titles like "clerk" and "stenographer" have given way to various types of "word processors." Some type, some file, some take dictation, some operate the word processing machines, but few do all these tasks. All this has brought about definite changes in hiring, using, and moving employees.

As we'll see later, one of the things we've discovered is that reducing the variety of the job in many cases decreases the amount of job satisfaction and hence also diminishes motivation. People are looking for meaningful work to do, and when we oversimplify or indulge in too much specialization, we almost always deduct something from the job satisfaction. What has actually happened, however, is that while some forces—usually for economic reasons—are doing away with the "generalist" concept, others are working within the organization to make the jobs more "enriched," hence going against the direction of the organization. Of course, each makes its impact, and the result is a changed organization that looks not exactly like either group really wanted. Rarely are the supervisors, especially at lower levels, aware of the tug-of-war that goes on, but at least some of the frustration, conflict and ambiguities filter down to them. The confusion, which is part of the problem in understanding how to supervise in today's work world, does little to make it any easier to supervise the new workers, especially since they may have come in with some suspicions about the confusion in the organization.

None of this should be interpreted as pessimism toward the possible success of the supervisor in today's business world; rather, as we look at the problem in more detail, it should be seen as additional information that will help us solve the mystery. (A batter needs to know how many strikes he has against him to know what to do with the next ball that is thrown!) The world of work has always been fraught with frustrations caused by paradoxes, inequities, and constant inroads made by seemingly insoluble problems. As time goes on, however, we get better and better at solving these kinds of problems. Anyone who thinks that the problems of thirty years ago were just as complex as today's doesn't understand the complexity of today's problems. The exciting thing about it for supervisors is that there *are* solutions; even though we know that there will always be difficulties, we can solve some and move on to others that are probably lurking just around the corner. Remember that the supervisor's job *isn't* to get the job done *after* all the confusion, frustration, and conflict in policies have been removed; it *is* to get the job done with whatever type of employee is provided in whatever kind of work situation. If all the problems were removed and if all the people were "ideal" and had the "right" attitudes, we might wonder why we even need supervisors in the first place.

LOSS OF AWARENESS

As organizations get bigger and more complex, and as management has more to concern itself about with regard to outside influences, another unfortunate thing happens: management loses an awareness of the individuals and their problems and concerns. While management is concerned with learning technological advances, meeting the competition for good employees, filling jobs with consideration to Equal Employment guidelines, and struggling to satisfy various directing groups, the individual gets lost. Only the supervisor can see the individual needs and the effect the organization has on the person. By this very "unawareness," management causes an increased turnover of employees who fail to feel a part of the organization, and thus it creates for itself the additional problem of losing sight of its employees' individual needs. Increased turnover means more new employees for management to get to know with fewer of them getting as much attention as they need, and the results are less awareness, less meeting of needs, and more turnover. Just as parents often try to satisfy their children by giving them material things instead of the less tangible but more important consideration of personal attention, organizations give the workers more benefits, more time off for holidays and vacations, but less and less attention. And just as children who get no personal attention grow up to have little respect for their parents, the worker who gets no personal attention ends up with even less regard for the organization than before.

Labor unions have always tried to show an interest in the individual, and indeed they will often go to bat for the individual who is seemingly wronged by the organization. In reality it is impossible for the unions or employee representation organizations ever to do anything for the individual except on a mass scale. Any benefits received on an individual basis are, in fact, being received by hundreds or thousands of others at the same time. Admittedly, the employee organizations can appear to give more individual attention, and hence get more credit for their interest, than can the management of the organization, and they rarely restrict their interest to justifiable causes. If a dues-paying member asks for help, regardless of the rightness or wrongness of the situation, the employee organization will at least give a sympathetic ear.

POLITICAL AND SOCIAL INFLUENCES

Remember, we are talking in this chapter about how the organizations have changed. Some of the changes have been the result of internal happenings, such as the changing face of the workers and the changing philosophies of managing. Some have been the result of external influences, such as unions and mergers. A significant external pressure for change has been the impact on the organization of the political and community reaction to words like "profit" and "record earnings." At one time these were a mark of success, and the community, government agencies, and local government figures would rejoice at such reports. It meant that the system of free enterprise and capitalism was working, that payrolls would be met, and that the community would flourish for another year. It was, indeed, a matter of pride in which all felt a share because the businesses were doing well. In the last several years, however, this has changed to the opposite extreme, especially when we consider the larger concerns. Many see bigness as bad and profit-making as antipatriotic. Where once the organizations were proud of a good, profitable year, they now may try to hide the figures in some way, showing "profit per share" rather than profit in millions or billions. Politicians may even use the figures against the companies, appealing to the masses against this bigness. While this in no way represents the entire country or all politicians, many organizations fear releasing figures at all lest the media or politicians show that information in a bad light. In some cases the organizations are in a squeeze with the separation between higher management and the hourly workers; instead of being proud of their organization, employees may think they're being cheated out of what should rightfully be theirs.

Part of the change these things have brought about in the organization is the development of a social "consciousness." Corporations that used to get good press by releasing glowing profit figures that showed how successful they had been over the past year now release annual reports filled with pictures of all the good things they contributed to the local communities. Now there are pictures of small children or hospitals where once there were pictures of expansion and assembly lines. Again, this isn't a universal trend, but it's prevalent and the reasons are obvious. How does this change affect the relationship between the organization and the hourly workers? There is no directly resulting feeling, and this lack in itself indicates that the social consciousness is producing nothing good *within* the organization, at least as far as the employees' attitude toward the organization is concerned. Seeing the reports of these things in the papers or in the financial reports may even work strongly against the good attitude the organization strived for. The employees, always needing more money because they never think they can live within their existing wages, see these "gifts to the community" as somehow coming out of their pockets. However, there is a very good chance that most of the organizations were already doing many things for the communities well in advance of these later public relations efforts but just didn't see any need to try to get "credit" for it. They were willing to do their part, saw needs, and contributed not only money but also the time of their employees, even of their executives; oddly enough, when the employees found out about it, they were proud rather than jealous or envious. Now organizations find themselves in a game that has either changing rules or no rules at all. And it's hard to win that kind of game.

While we have no need here to try to justify or condemn bigness or to decide whether it contributes to the community, we do need to say that top management has its hands full trying to second-guess the press and politicians. In all this guessing, it is easy to overlook the problems of the lower levels of supervision and the hourly workers. As a matter of fact, without having the information that top management has, it is easy for them to misunderstand top management's problems and actions. To make matters worse, even if higher management were aware of what all this has done to the lower levels of the organization, they could hardly let their hair down and reveal all their motives and efforts at second-guessing. The gap in understanding and communications appears and continues to get wider, and everybody *seemingly* works to make it wider while saying they would like to narrow it. Although there is no doubt that they *would* like to narrow the gap (when and if they are fully aware of it), it remains; the task of serving in the interface role always falls to the first level of supervision. They must represent the organization and try to explain policies they don't understand and didn't have any part in setting. As we have already established, the problem is compounded by the fact that the newer employees aren't likely to try too hard to be tolerant; they are likely to be pretty demanding for answers that aren't going to be there for them. This, too, adds some coal to the fire of change within the organization.

COMPETITION HAS CHANGED

With the advent of spiraling inflation, profits have often been narrowed, and competition has become stiffer. At the same time, a caution flag has been raised about being too aggressive, and much of the competition battle has been waged with gloves on. Truth-in-advertising regulations have caused all kinds of change in advertising styles. Employees sit at home and watch television advertisements in which movie stars extol the virtues of the products they (the employees) work on everyday, but they feel no particular relationship to the product or the organization. The skeptical workers, who have grown to recognize hypocrisy better than any other generation, feel no pride in their product, but rather ridicule what's being said about it. Since they don't have the company loyalty that previous generations had, they rarely think beyond their own working conditions and their own supervision. If they have a bad boss, they think of the whole organization as being bad, and *it's not hard to understand why.* We lack perception and sensitivity if we can't see that they were brought up and trained to think just the way they do.

We understand, of course, that television advertising isn't aimed at the employees of the organization that produced the item being advertised, but we are pointing out that there are people with different kinds of attitudes and values watching the commercials and that almost anything the organization does may be seen as suspect by the employees. It is also likely that the employees watching the competition's commercials may compare and rate their product higher than their own. The built-in ability to be critical may be the cause of this. We need to remember that one of the basic characteristics of these newer working people is their ability to be perfectly at ease speaking against things they don't like, no matter how "sacred" the subject might be. These new workers have been brought up in a climate where everyone wanted to hear everything they had to say, and it would never occur to them not to speak their opinion. The fact that "it just isn't done" makes no sense to them. If they think it, why not say it!

One of the problems that bothers the generation of the 1960s forward is the practice of what they perceive as hypocrisy. They saw their parents in situations they thought were hypocritical, they saw their teachers in the same light, and they even thought that their religion was tainted with hypocrisy. Closer examination sometimes showed them that there were circumstances that made things *seem* more hypocritical than they really were; unfortunately, sometimes they found that hypocrisy really was there. Too often their parents, teachers, or religious leaders either refused to admit it, shrugged their shoulders and said "someday you'll understand," or admitted it and said that this is just the way it is in the real world. Then they themselves came into the *real world* and found that the newspapers were full of stories about "collusion," "price setting," and under-the-table dealings among businesses. They learned about the government's antitrust suits that were trying to break up the big conglomerates and big monopolies, and they interpreted such news reports to mean that business was all bad. With a lack of trust learned very early in life, they found it easy to accept what they read and apply it to *all* businesses, even the business they were working for.

As a result of the bad reports, organizations were changing and were making these changes felt down the line. The levels of management stressed rules about not taking favors from clients or from suppliers, but by the time they got to the hourly workers, their importance had been lost in the urgency of the production requirements, deadlines, shortages, or overtaking the competition. Higher management was finding other ways to get the favors needed (or at least thought needed) and giving the organization a different appearance. Frequently, this came across as only another problem of bigness.

REGULATORY PRESSURES

Perhaps nothing in the life of organizations in this country has had the same impact as and caused as much change as government regulation. In a relatively short time, organizations have found themselves flooded with federal, state, and local government regulations that pertain to almost every aspect of the activities they engage in. There are regulations for employing, promoting, firing, unionizing, safety, and anything connected with the environment. These external regulations could have been predicted, because they came as a result of the organizations' oversights, lack of interest, or failure to regulate themselves in the things now being regulated. Since no one likes to be told what they can and can't do, the regulations were naturally resented, and—as is always the case with external regulation—there were inequities, discrepancies, and many, many forms to be filled out. Since there was no way to get out from under the regulations and nothing to do but conform and fill out the endless reports, businesses and other organizations changed their behavior, their image, or their viewpoints. Sometimes the change showed contempt for the rules; sometimes it altered the organization enough to remove it from some of the regulations; and sometimes it added more people to fight the regulations and do as little as possible to conform. The end result was that even less time was available to give to understanding the new workers.

Along with this pressure from regulation, there entered another factor that fit right in with the philosophy of the new workers: the matter of "rights." In the middle 1960s, the rights issue pertained mostly to discrimination against minorities, but it spread to every part of the society. The generation that entered their teens in the late sixties were caught up in all kinds of "rights" questions, including the right not to fight a war they thought was unjustified. Although it wasn't limited to this generation, the struggle spread to the college campuses and became a more integral part of their thinking than was true with any other single age group. It certainly was not a part of the philosophy of the older generation who were to be the supervisors of the new work force, but it did become something for businesses to consider. Management decisions were constantly flavored by what effect the decisions would have on the people and their perceived rights. Every job description, every reorganization of people and work assignments, and every change or promotion had to be preceded by a consideration of the way the moves would be interpreted, even when the people affected probably would never think of it.

This new necessity of consideration brought about a dual pressure. There was the ever-present pressure from the regulatory agencies, which were gradually gaining enforcement powers and winning actions against organizations for alleged discrimination or violation of individual rights. There was also pressure from within the organization from the people who might think their rights were being violated. Obvious moves that would seem to be in the best interest of good business and all the people concerned were sometimes not made; instead, management made less understandable moves, promoting people or changing jobs when it didn't make sense, even to the people involved. To complicate the problem, moves made for the reasons we're talking about couldn't be explained in terms of the real reasons. Organizations just couldn't say, "This doesn't look like the best move, but we're doing this so nobody will feel like their rights have been violated!" The reasons given made less sense, and often put the organizations in a bad light vis à vis their employees. A further complication was that, even when the moves were not made on the basis of fear of discrimination but for totally sound business and practical reasons, those who didn't like the decisions or who felt they'd been overlooked (not discriminated against, just overlooked by another candidate for a different or higher job), *thought* they were made because of the pressures just mentioned. Even if they were told the logic of the move, they often shrugged and said, "Yeah, I know, I know it" even if they really didn't.

While management was trying unskillfully to put out fires to avoid trouble with the newly imposed regulations, but getting little help from the regulatory forces, along came a new work force brought up to defend the rights of anybody and everybody, including themselves. Remember, this is the group that had been trained to get instant gratification for their wants; just as they wanted equality on the campus or an *immediate* change in anything that didn't make sense, they expected the same kind of action from their employers. It was difficult for them to see why organizations didn't immediately handle the regulations for cleaning up their air, the rivers, or the airways. Any delay was seen as something the organization was doing in order to avoid doing what it was supposed to do. As it turned out, it was not a very good frame of mind with which to understand management's changes and actions.

There were more changes; the pressures from both outside and within added another dimension that hadn't existed before. It meant that supervisors at all levels, especially at lower levels, had to be trained *not to violate the regulations.* Training time is always hard to come by, and the time for training first levels of supervision is perhaps the most difficult to find because there are more supervisors at this level than at any other. Next, since training time is scarce, using what little there is for such subjects as how to deal with OSHA and EEOC problems often eliminates time that could otherwise be spent teaching how to supervise the hourly workers. The irony is that there is probably more time spent now in training the first-level supervisors than ever before, but at the sacrifice of supervisory skills. It's not hard for a training director to manage to get a week of training for all supervisors if the subject is how to keep from violating some regulation or how to implement the new affirmative action program, but it is much more difficult to get the same amount of time for a course in everyday supervisory skills.

Again, none of the things said so far apply to all organizations, and nothing is intended to defend or refute the regulations or the regulating agencies. It's just important to note how organizations and the relationship between management and the new workers have changed as a result of various pressures.

"The way I read the regulation, we can't build a working model until we've demonstrated on a working model that a model will work."

MORE KNOWLEDGE ABOUT PEOPLE

In the face of all the things that have caused the organizations' communications efforts to be less effective, we find that we know more about people than ever before. We know more about how to motivate people, how to make them enjoy their jobs, and how to use responsibility and recognition as motivating tools. We know more than ever before about what causes conflict and interpersonal problems and more about how to solve them. We know about different kinds of management styles and what to expect from each kind. We know how to predict behavior a little better than in years gone by, and we know something about how different people will react to different actions. Even with all this information, however, we're often less able to use it than ever before, because we're so busy with the other things mentioned in this chapter.

In addition to not being able to find the time, the big problem confronting the people trying to pass this knowledge on to the supervisors is that the new workers have made such an impact (mostly unfavorable) on the experienced supervisors that they aren't nearly as receptive as they otherwise would be. Survey after survey of the older supervisors reveals that they think the new workers are unmanageable, uninterested in work, disloyal, and unstable. They also think that the new employees are looking for an easy way to make a lot of money, want to move up to higher jobs without waiting their turn, and become impatient when they are assigned routine jobs that have to be done at their level in the organization. They see the new workers as unwilling to take direction, unwilling to be subordinate, uninterested in overtime, and more interested in their outside activities than anything about the job. While there are all kinds of exceptions to these opinions, they still hold for the majority of the old-line supervisors. Many either secretly or openly believe the solution is to change all these people to think "like we do or get out!" Many believe that the time is going to come when things will be "like they used to be," or when personnel departments will stop hiring "this kind of people." The many who don't believe this take an equally useless approach, that "things will never get any better, so I'll just wait out my retirement and chuck the whole thing."

It becomes difficult to try to persuade people with such attitudes that good supervision is still the answer to the problem. To suggest that they can apply the things we know about people to this present work force is sheer folly to many of them. They readily admit that they need help, but they are not that ready to admit that the solutions offered will actually get the job done. For people who train these supervisors, it becomes essential to talk in terms of reality; textbook solutions or academic theories, so designated, will fall on deaf ears. The truth is, many have gone so far into the "depths of despair" over the problem that they may never really listen as they should. Because of their loyalty to the organization, commitment to anybody working for them, and desire to do their jobs correctly, the good supervisors will see the value of trying to save the people working for them. These good supervisors make up the majority of those on the job, so it is to them that a book like this must be directed.

CONCLUSION

In our little mystery drama, we've added to the confusion by showing not only that we have a new kind of employee working for us, but that we also have the complexity of a changing organization. The new-generation employee thinks and acts differently, and his or her new value system directly conflicts with the existing values of supervisors. The organizations have changed, not to conform to this new value system, but because of many things altogether separate from this. In many cases, the changes have only widened the gap. The supervisors who are trying to get the job done with today's work force are doing it with constrictions never before encountered. In many ways, the problem of the new worker is seen as minor compared with the pressures and problems brought about by public image problems, regulation, and political pressures and changing times that are the result of an accumulation of many things. The pressures are so real that dealing with difficult workers gets low priority at top management levels; in fact, it many not even get on the priority list.

Where does this leave the immediate supervisor of the new and different work force? All the clichés fit: up the creek without a paddle; on the spot; between a rock and a hard place. The solution isn't easy. It will take commitment and some hard, concentrated thought about a very serious and complex problem. Most of all, it will take a positive attitude that not only *says* it can be solved but *believes* it can. Another clue (which ties in with the first one given in Chapter 1): Since we do know a lot about people, and since basic human nature doesn't really change, we add to this the knowledge we have of the people now working for us. We use them against themselves, so to speak. Maybe this sounds complicated, but we certainly won't solve the problem just by taking what we know about people in general and applying it to *our value system.* While human nature doesn't change, value systems do. We will find the answer when we have looked at this new value system and applied our knowledge to it. It will take an open mind and a willingness to try some things that may appear a bit risky, but willingness to take a risk is what supervision is all about. After all, what's the difference between willingness to take *responsibility* and willingness to take *risks?*

DISCUSSION QUESTIONS

1. List reasons, other than workers' attitudes, that the role of supervision has so drastically changed.
2. Discuss how public image, regulation, and political pressures have affected the organization.
3. What is responsible for causing the greatest impact and change in the organization?
4. How did the "personal rights" philosophy fit in with the regulatory pressures?
5. Where is the immediate supervisor in all of these difficulties? How can the supervisor use his or her knowledge of human nature to help solve the problems?

part two

Approaches to Supervision

Chapter three

How Do Supervisory Styles Develop?

When we look at the various ways today's supervisors work and try to unravel the complex problem of supervising today's work force, we need to understand a few things about ourselves, including the fact that the particular style we are using is the result of one or more of the following factors:

1. We supervise like our bosses supervised us.
2. We supervise like we were taught to do in the books we've read or the training courses we've had.
3. We supervise in a way that seems natural to us without thinking about it at all.

We need to examine and test the reliability of each of these factors. First, if we are copying our bosses, we should know that each of them supervises with methods that result from training, experience, trial and error, and a bit of the three things mentioned above. Next, if we follow what we read or were taught about supervision, we must recognize that those ideas are a combination of what was available to the writer or the trainer, what was popular at the time, what the originator liked (or believed), what was knowledge or theory at the time, and what management wanted to be taught. Finally, as we'll see later in this chapter, supervision is too complicated for us to be lucky enough to just fall into all things good by accident or by doing what comes naturally. In other words, it is a skill, and people don't succeed at many complicated things without planned effort.

In every case just mentioned, the styles being practiced were based on *history,* not on the results of present-day, ongoing research. Though research is continuing, it will take a while for it to become a part of our daily lives. Because researchers are under strict restraints to *time-test* their ideas, it takes a considerable time for even a proven idea to make its way into practice. To make today's work world more complicated for us, there is probably much less research in this field going on now than in the past, and even those results will take some time to get to us.

Still, we need to see how we arrived at today's various supervisory styles, theories, and practices. In this chapter, we'll see how theories get to be practice and where some of them came from. In addition, we'll look at styles of supervision, management, and leadership. By seeing where we've come from, we may be able to see more clearly where we're going.

WHERE THEORIES COME FROM

One problem we have when we try to set up some standards for supervision is that we end up calling principles "theories," which most people think of as unproven

ideas. They think that if a thing is still a theory, it lacks validity and shouldn't be taken too seriously. Perhaps because supervision is less than an exact science, people
can't quite bring themselves to make a list of things that
are known for sure about supervising people. (We might
have been better off years ago, when we started thinking
about the art and science of supervision, if we had used
words like "principles" or "rules" instead of "theories."
That way there might have been more credibility in books
such as this one!) Obviously, one way to make it easier to
accept what we know about supervisor-subordinate relationships is to redefine the word "theory." Without looking
for a dictionary definition, let's just say that for the most
part "theory," as the word is used in supervision, refers to a
group of basic *assumptions* that have had enough exposure in the real world to qualify as facts. The science isn't
quite rigid or stringent enough to see an exact point where
the principle changes from assumption into unquestioned
truth.

There is always a need for basic "assumptions," because they don't just happen. As we'll see in a moment,
assumptions have a high degree of acceptability because
they are based on a great deal of reliable data and have
been tested in the real world. As long as the assumption is
based on documented results from many areas—or at
least from the area in which we're trying to operate—we
must accept them until something better comes along.
Most of the assumptions about people are pretty well sub-
stantiated since they usually come from people who not
only have the background to understand the research
they're doing, but also have had the opportunity to devote
time, energy, and study to building a base for the assumptions. These proponents usually have a reputation, and to
protect that reputation they often go beyond routine research to make certain there are no flaws in what they're

saying. Few unknown people with no reputation in the field have contributed much to the basic assumptions about supervision. Those who have contributed have waited a long time for the acceptance that came only after the more reputable people experimented with the idea and found it to be valid.

For the most part, the principles of supervision that are accepted today come from social scientists or industrial psychologists, who have the time and inclination to do research in the field and who are under the same constraints as any scientist. They must undertake tedious experimentation in "laboratory" conditions, which are most often found in the real business world. If they want to know how certain kinds of actions produce certain suspected reactions, they set up conditions that allow that action and whatever reaction that will result. They carefully arrange the conditions so that no external influences will taint the picture, and they repeat it again and again until there is no doubt about the result. The researchers aren't graduate students writing about one short observation of twenty people; they are performing research that will prove as conclusively as possible that when supervisors do certain things they can expect *specific* results from *most of the people* working under them.

These researchers must follow all the rules of the game and even withstand pretty strong opposition when they present their findings, especially if their conclusions fly in the face of existing thought or belief. This means that they must have an adequate *sample* of typical *people* under controlled *conditions* that are free from the possibility of *incorrect findings.* Then there must be the final test: Can others reproduce the results? No assumption is likely to get into classrooms, textbooks, or general practice unless it can be validated by other researchers who try to get the same results under the same conditions. If all this sounds like the chemistry or biology lab, the point has been made well. Certainly, some researchers who have developed untested theories over the years have gotten some recognition, but usually they have used the results others have obtained through extensive research to come up with a hypothesis that gets attention. In all fairness to the whole field, it is probably more accurate to say that the researchers who only theorize from others' findings *get quoted more than used!*

It can be seen from all this that it's hard to get much information into practice, considering the restrictions on quality and the time it takes to obtain valid results. But there is yet another barrier. Very few researchers are interested in the broad spectrum of the supervisor-subordinate relationship, because it would be impossible to cover the whole area even if they were to devote their whole life's research to it. Both their interests and the restrictions usually confine them to a smaller area of research. Although it might appear as though they've looked at the whole field of management and come up with findings about all the expected results from such things as authoritative versus participative management, such isn't the case. Usually they've studied only one small area and then made a broad application. To be sure, their application has much merit, because they mix the research done with live people with the results of other research and come up with a fairly good, overall set of assumptions. As they expect, however, this broad-brush treatment is open to question, and sometimes their findings are never quite accepted. Acceptance always comes easier if the findings seem to support what we have always suspected; if they don't, there is much less readiness to go along blindly.

To confound the matter further, researchers are working in narrow areas that may leave gaps in our knowledge when we try to fit everything together. Or just as often they may overlap, not enough to be completely parallel, but skewed enough to be different. Although there may be no apparent discrepancies, there certainly will be questionable areas and a lack of total information. Taking this matter of gaps and overlaps together with all the other things said so far, one cannot help but wonder how it is we know anything for sure about supervising people. Fortunately, many people have been at it for a long time and have given us a great deal of useful information. The only shortcoming we have is that it takes a long time to go from research to practice, which means that even though there is much research going on with the new work force, it will be a while yet before we have all the information we need to do the job properly. As has been said several times, much—if not most—of what we've found out about people in the past will apply to these new workers, too.

While we're talking about gaps, let's close one. So far we have created a mystery of sorts by saying that we have a new generation of people whose value system doesn't match that of the existing organization or supervision and then by saying that human nature doesn't change and that people are always people. If this is so, what is the problem? Why is there a gap in our ability to learn about how to supervise this new generation? One of the reasons we have so much trouble teaching about them is that we are still using the examples of yesteryear instead of up-to-date examples. We talk about people wanting responsibility and then use an example from the time when workers were less educated and more willing to do anything just for recognition. There was a time when just allowing them to "hold the wrench" was a great deal of responsibility, but we must find something else to use as an example of responsibility with this younger group of people. We talk about the use of discipline and refer to a three-day suspension. That would have worked a few years ago, but now the worker may just say, "Fine. Make it Wednesday, Thursday, and Friday, since I'm off already Monday and Tuesday." Obviously, then, these new workers will require us to find other means of discipline, which we will discuss as we work through the intricacies of the puzzle before us. That's why it was said in the last chapter that it may be a little scary for some of us to see the way we'll have to go.

DANGERS OF IMITATION

As already said, imitation is another source of supervisory style. Just because we don't have anything else to go by, we follow the apparent style of our bosses, even though that approach has all kinds of fairly apparent fallacies. We are supervising like our bosses, who did a good job of supervising us, but *our people aren't like we were,* and even our good bosses would not have been successful with the new work force if they used the methods they did with us. Note the words "apparent style of our bosses." Chances are good that we can completely misunderstand someone else's style if we aren't certain of the reasons for his or her behavior, especially when we are actually the recipients of that supervision. We may be able to understand what our bosses were doing, but since we probably didn't understand ourselves very well at that time, we still have a problem. To say the least, trying to imitate a style under those conditions is foolhardy.

Another problem with imitation is that the chances are good that sometimes we not only didn't understand the bosses we had, but also *didn't even like what they were doing.* If we forget those times and imitate our bosses, our workers may not be dissatisfied, but we'll be pretty lucky if they are ecstatic! The problem is that we aren't capable at this late date to separate what we liked or disliked about the style our bosses used. It starts to run together at some point, and we end up trying to imitate something that is at best nebulous, and at worst totally lost. Thus we would do well to find some way to supervise other than copying.

We can carry it further, too. Not only did the bosses fail to reveal to us the reasons for their actions, but there were many times when they didn't even know themselves why they did what they did. Styles aren't things we carry around in a sack, readily available for examination by one and all, including ourselves, and none of us is good enough to get a style so down pat that we know every reason for everything we do. If somebody questions us, we may give a made-up answer, we may give an opinion, or we may just say we don't know. If we imitate the boss, and the boss didn't know why he or she was doing something a certain way, we are at least guilty of perpetuating nonreasoning.

If we follow the bosses' patterns, we may be in further trouble because the bosses we've had may have gotten their ideas from *unreliable sources,* and there is nothing to make us believe that when they first became supervisors they had sources of information any better than ours on how to supervise. Let's look at how people learn to supervise. Remember, we're talking not only about the boss, but also about ourselves a few years ago.

Trial and Error

It's Monday and I'm a new supervisor as of today. What do supervisors do? On Monday morning, I'll have to start the doing before I figure out what they do. Assignments have to be made; questions must be answered; some people won't show up; substitutions have to be made; production starts and people are asking what to do; the boss is asking me how things are going. I don't know, and even though I haven't figured out for sure what supervisors are supposed to be doing, I'm busy supervising. I am, in fact, much involved in trial-and-error supervision under poor laboratory conditions.

Common Sense

When I've been on the job longer and problems arise, I see myself doing what common sense tells me. I become very wise in my ignorance. I presume people are certain ways, then act accordingly. We like to think of "common sense" as using good judgment, but this isn't right unless we have facts, knowledge, and experience to build that sense up to a usable level. Back to the chemistry lab again: It might make good sense or seem logical that, if I mix a clear liquid with a red one, I'll get a pale yellow one. Without knowledge of chemical reactions, I might think that this is the case, but in fact I could get almost any color, from black to clear to in-between, depending on the substances I use. So it is with common sense.

Imitation

Many hazards are involved in doing what somebody else has done. Different people, different jobs, different personalities, different circumstances, and different times make imitation a less-than-satisfactory method. Imitation may be a sincere form of flattery, but it is a poor way to develop a supervisory style.

Doing What Comes Naturally

There is little difference between common sense or trial and error. We just roll with the punches, react in a way that "feels" good, and know we're right because of the way we feel. Of all the methods of supervising, this one is the one most likely to be used by most people, even after they've been around awhile. Example: I'm in my office or at my work station and an employee comes up for an assignment. I suggest the work that needs to be done and tell the person in as nice a voice as I have, but instead of responding positively, the employee gets loud and almost hostile and throws the work order down on the desk. What do I do if I function according to the "doing what comes naturally" method? If I respond to the employee in the same tone, I'm probably doing the natural thing . . . but I'm wrong!

Situation Supervision

In this we do whatever the situation seems to demand, without thinking about it. It is sometimes called *contingency management,* but actually that term applies only when we know what the alternatives are and why we're doing what the situation demands. It is really *crisis management*—reaction instead of action. We're letting the situation control us rather than controlling it. The sad part about it is that many people spend a lifetime supervising without doing anything else. They're inept, often confused, and the worst part of it is that it's a good way to ruin a lot of potentially good people.

Training

Of all the choices, this method is the most likely to succeed. At least we get the benefit of other people's thoughts and research and a chance to see several alternatives and to test our own ideas. As we'll see in more detail in the next section, training has its drawbacks, but its saving factor is that even though we may end up imitating the training source, we can have some confidence in that source. We have to believe that the styles being encouraged have at least a basis in truth and that they're at least more organized than our own confused beginnings.

CAN WE TRUST OUR TRAINING?

How did supervisory training programs come into existence and how good are they? For the most part, practically every training effort is a direct result of some kind of training effort that has been in existence for some time. It may be one that is "warmed over," or maybe even "warmed up," but it usually has some history in the organization, either as a program once intended for another segment of the supervisory forces or as a continuation of the exact program that's been used all along, with only the instructions changed. All this isn't necessarily bad, but the program may not suit the supervisors' present needs. As we saw in the last section, the examples may be out of date and even the material may be somewhat antiquated. Although the material may still be relevant, it is a poor justification of a training program to say that it is part or all of the existing program because "we've always taught supervision this way."

Training programs may also come into being through some available "packages" on the market that are all ready to go, requiring little or no effort of the trainers. For the most part, these are "shelf packages"; they can be bought right off the shelf and plugged into almost any organization, be it an insurance company, a federal agency, or a chain of food stores. Some are even franchised, in that the company that has developed the programs will train the trainers and then, under a royalty system, furnish the material to train every supervisor. Are these programs any good? A later section of this chapter will discuss how to test them; in general, it is fair to say that they are usually well developed and that they deal with general aspects of supervision. For the most part, they do not cover specific problems, and few of them deal at all with the problem of supervising the younger workers. It is also fairly safe to say that virtually none of these programs have ever been validated within the organization purchasing the program and rarely get validated by the in-house trainers. Therefore there is a danger in this approach if we expect to solve specific supervisory problems within our own organization, especially if our problems are unique to our organization or to our particular kind of operation within the industry or government.

In a similar manner, we also get training programs when we hire outside consultants, who conduct supervisory courses. Some who have experience in conducting various kinds of training programs will come into the office and do the training. But because they may work for one government agency one week, another the next, a pharmaceutical company the next, and then go on to an oil company, a city government group, and a textile mill, we may again be dealing with generalities versus specifics. The consultants usually have several things in their favor: they have had experience in supervision, they have taken time to study the available material on supervision, and they devote much if not all of their time to doing so. They usually have a core course already available and can customize it for almost any kind of supervisory group. And, being outsiders, they may get more respect than one of the men or women within the organization who tells the supervisors how to supervise. Consultants can also draw from experiences they have had or heard about in different places they have worked. The list may go on, but this gives an idea of reasons for hiring a consultant to handle training.

As attractive as the list sounds, though, there are many handicaps and drawbacks to using an outside consultant. No matter how good the consultants are, they are still outsiders and cannot relate exactly to the problems within an organization. They can neither speak for the higher management of the organization nor answer policy questions. They may be just parroting something they've said many, many times, while losing sight of the deficiencies within the organization they have been called in to serve. In terms of the cost of using a training staff as an alternative, consultants are expensive (though not as much when figured on a per-head-trained basis). Some consultants who are in great demand because they have developed a good stage presentation, do not try to familiarize themselves with the organization's goals, problems, routines, or policies, and end up doing a stand-up routine instead of handling down-to-earth training. Since they catch the first plane out of town and never see the results of their efforts, they do not have to live with their training. A few try to sell their own products and build up a need for their further services, but they do not necessarily make this known in the original agreement. The list can go on, but we can see from these few factors that some genuine, difficult problems are involved in hiring an outside consultant. As far as dealing with the present-day work force is concerned, most consultants who have made themselves well enough known to be in demand, got their actual supervisory experience before the problem became significant. This leads to the danger of getting not a practitioner but a theorist, who knows what the book says but has never tried it out in the real world.

Another source of training programs is top management

when it issues edicts about when the training will be done, who will do it, and, most importantly, *what will be included in the training program.* Most trainers long for the day when top management will show an interest in training and give it official sanction or real support by allocating money in the budget, authorizing space for training, and assigning people to have exclusive training responsibilities. Sometimes the support exceeds this, though, and trainers are assigned the actual subjects. However, unless top management has close contact with the workers and knows their nature pretty well, this can be almost disastrous. As we have seen, things change from the time top managers got to where they are in the organization, and time dampens memory even if there hasn't been much change. Top managers might decree that a course be conducted on "communications" because they have discovered that some of their messages are apparently not getting through, whereas the real problem might be that the lower levels of the organization are very frustrated because these messages *are* getting through but run counter to the needs of the organization at this level. The first-line supervisors who try to carry out the policies discussed in the messages meet resistance from the workers and are held in disdain by the other supervisors. Top management seldom decrees that first-level supervisors be trained how to deal with the new attitudes and problems brought in by the younger employees, and it is doubtful that many at the top level even know that such attitudes exist, since indeed *they didn't exist* when they were at a lower level.

Finally, the training the boss got or the training that is available to us may be just the result of certain biases or pets of the person who conducts the organization's training programs. These may or may not apply to the problems we might be having in supervising the new work force, just as they may or may not have applied when our bosses

"*I'm telling you right now, we're going to have participative manage-ment around here whether the people want it or not!*"

were trained. Because chances are good that trainers will be busy just trying to meet the requirements of the various regulations placed on them by OSHA, EEOC, etc., they may not have enough time to develop a program that deals only with how to supervise the new workers. Dealing with a subject as nebulous as this may not be a high-priority item; it certainly wasn't when our bosses got their training.

So what has been said so far about training? We started off by trying to figure out how we and our bosses were trained, and in each case we've seen that more than likely the training inadvertently avoided the issue of how to deal with the new workers. We've seen how we get the supervisory training; now let's see how we can tell if it's the right training. What will be said here deals with supervisory training of any kind, not just training aimed at dealing with the new work force, for supervisors need to know many more things besides that. If we've established anything so far, it is that human nature fortunately stays the same and that any supervisory training must include information about dealing with people. Most of this isn't going to vary much from generation to generation.

How can we tell if the training we're getting is the kind we need or if it is valuable to us? We can give some tests and ask some questions that will let us know just how much value there is to the training and will give us a very good measure of the training's worth.

1. Is the training designed for supervisors like me? "Like me" means supervisors in the same kind of environment as I work in. If the training is aimed at supervisors who have the same general education level as I, and is pitched at this level, it will more likely suit me as far as the level of the approach is concerned. Also, it needs to be aimed at supervisors who have the same degree of latitude, authority, and responsibility as I have. If I have no latitude in making certain kinds of decisions, then the course won't help me if it presumes that everybody can make certain decisions that are beyond me. While the training doesn't necessarily have to be just for people engaged in exactly the same kind of work I'm in, it helps if there is at least a similarity. If I'm a manager of a branch bank and most of the training concerns supervision on the night shift of a steel plant, there obviously may be some shortcomings in the training.

2. Is the training designed for supervisors of people like mine? The training should be not only for supervisors like me, but it should deal with people like those who report to me. If all the examples involve women in an office steno pool and I supervise a group of laborers in a paper plant, I can't identify nearly as readily. Further, the content should also be aimed at dealing with problems encountered by supervisors who oversee the kind of people I do, and certainly the course should be up-to-date as far as the way it deals with my kind of people. If my people are unionized, the issues and answers should be couched in union terms, rather than in ways I cannot translate to fit my situation. If my people aren't organized and have no plans to consider such action, the training should deal with problems encountered in nonunion environments. If not, I can't relate to it very well.

3. Has this training program worked elsewhere? If the training program has been used somewhere else, it needs to be checked to see that it really did train supervisors to do their jobs better. Supervisors saying they like the course does not validate it; there should be some kind of concrete evidence that people are actually performing their jobs more effectively as a result of their training. If we have this kind of information, we are in much better shape when it is used again, especially if it's used with the same kind of supervisors.

4. Will it be supported by my supervision/management? This does not mean whether my higher management will allow the training to proceed, but whether it will allow the training to be applied back on the job. If I take the training, will my supervisor tell me to forget it? If so, then the training obviously isn't meeting my needs; if I'm not reinforced by my supervisor, I'm not going to make much effort to apply it. Further, if I fear that my boss isn't going to like what I'm being trained to do, I won't put much effort into the training program itself. More than likely, I'll just be a problem for the trainer. For a training program to be good and worthwhile from the organization's standpoint, higher management must support it.

5. Does it represent my organization's style? It's not much of a training program if it teaches one kind of supervision while my organization practices another. If the course is teaching me how to practice participative management and is giving me all the tools to do so while practically everyone in higher levels of management uses a very autocratic style, the course may even be harmful. If I practice this newly learned skill, I'm going against organizational standards; if I don't use it, I'll be frustrated, especially if the trainer convinced me that this kind of management is the best. If I take a good course in delegation skill and my organization—as represented by my immediate supervisor—expects me to do all the work myself and delegate practically nothing, then I become frustrated. Such a training course would not be very valuable.

6. Can I use it directly and immediately? I must consider two things: Can I use the training as soon as I return, and can I use it without modifying it? First, if the course is only a look at some theories that are being considered but not planned for immediate use, I can't consider that the organization got its money's worth from my attendance. Even though the course teaches some useful skill or information, it will be of little use if I have to modify it. I need to get current and relevant information so I can go back to work, take off my coat, look at my people, and start applying what I've learned to the first problem that arises. This is asking a lot, but since my problems are real, the training ought to be real, too. If not, I can use the time better back on the job learning by trial and error.

These questions are guidelines that anyone can use to evaluate the worth of a training program. We can look at our own training and answer the question, "Can I trust my training?" because we have a set of real guidelines to follow.

THE FALLACY OF A DO-IT-YOURSELF STYLE

We've already seen that most people develop their own style, often without training. Let's take a look at how they develop a style, then see in more detail what's wrong with doing so.

1. Common sense approach. We've already learned the problem with this by observing that "common sense" needs to be educated.

2. "Doing what comes naturally" approach. As we've seen, doing what comes *un*naturally is often the best approach. What is natural for one person may be unnatural for another.

3. Experimental observation approach. This is fine, but only *if* we have enough time to make the observations scientifically before the walls crumble around us.

4. Trial-and-error approach. The very fact that we have to make errors for this method to work makes it suspect. Errors are costly, and if we have to run several people off or ruin several people's morale before we figure out what's wrong with our approach, we're in trouble.

5. "Wait for enough time" approach. Going ahead with supervising while we wait for enough spare time to learn about supervision may sound far out, but many people do it. Obviously, we never get the time, and it's just as well, because by the time we start our training, the bad habits we've picked up will be too strong for us to "unlearn" them.

6. Letting our people train us. If we could have heard our people talking about us when we first came on board, we'd have heard them using *exactly those words.* Remember, they've had more experience at being supervised than we've had at supervising. They'll train us if we give them a chance, and although the results will probably please them, they won't please us in the long run.

Thus we can see that there are some real fallacies in trying to develop our own supervisory style. The answer is that while many supervisors tend to develop their own style by one or more of the preceding processes, the procedure involves many pitfalls and very few advantages. Often it takes too long and the end product isn't worth the wait. Almost any alternative we can find to waiting until we get our own style (by whatever process) must be better than this do-it-yourself approach.

CONCLUSION

This chapter has discussed ways of learning supervisory styles and finding out about supervising people. From all this we've seen many alternatives and processes for developing styles of supervision, and also that supervisory "theories" have validity and a good basis in fact, because they're developed by people who are governed by the rules of scientific research. We've run into the hazards of dealing with the tendency to imitate bosses and their styles and have talked about the need to be cautious in using their approach to supervision since they didn't come by theirs in a very skillful way. We have seen that, for the most part, we should obtain skill at supervising from a training program; and that while all these training programs can't be trusted, we can ask some questions to test the worth of the programs. No matter where they come from, if they pass the tests, they have good information.

In spite of all this, however, there's a good chance that the training programs won't deal in any depth with how to supervise the newer workers, so we still haven't solved our problem. We are closer, however, for in these training programs we'll see the ways that people are alike, regardless of the age in which they live. If we can take this information and apply some of the rules to be pointed out in this book, we're far ahead of the game. In the remaining part of this book, we'll see what it is we will learn in these training programs as we study about human nature; as we do, we'll also find the keys to unlocking the mystery of supervising the younger generation of workers. As you read the ideas introduced, remember that this is a good chapter to come back to for an evaluation of the material presented. The same tests that are suggested here to measure the worth of any training program are valid for measuring the suggestions made in this book. If the things said aren't relevant and immediately usable, then the mystery we've started isn't going to have a very good ending. That would be unfair to you, though, so you can rest assured that the suggestions have already passed the tests. Still, you should check them out just the same.

DISCUSSION QUESTIONS

1. List the factors that determine our supervisory styles.

2. Discuss the meaning of "theory" as used in supervision. Where do the theories come from?

3. What are the hazards of "imitation" as a source of supervisory style?

4. Why will "doing what comes naturally" fail as an effective style?

5. Which is the best method for developing supervisory style and skill?

6. List different sources of supervisory training.

7. How can we determine if the training we're getting is the kind we need—if it will be of value to us?

8. What guidelines can we use to evaluate the worth of a training program?

9. What are the fallacies in developing each of the following "do-it-yourself" styles?

    a. Common sense approach

    b. Doing what comes naturally

    c. Wait for enough time

    d. Letting our people train us

Chapter four

Developing a
Supervisory Style

The one thing that has been repeated more than anything else so far in this book is that human nature doesn't really change with time. Even though people may develop different attitudes and value systems, they have a side that stays constant and their nature is such that we can even predict what some of their reactions will be. This chapter will start to point out some things that people have in common and try to answer the question, "What do we know for sure about people?" This becomes very critical because it is this *likeness* that will help solve the mystery of how to supervise the younger working people, with their "different" value systems and attitudes.

Before going into that, though, some things need to be understood. We need to know what people are like and how we can predict their behavior so we can develop a *style* of supervision that will help us in our day-to-day dealings with people. The moment we introduce the idea of a "style" we have a problem, though, because supervisors begin to get the idea that there is one way—and only one way—to supervise people. We need to avoid that concept if we possibly can, for it will lead us down some dangerous paths. If we become good enough at predicting behavior from the various ways we treat people, we can begin to treat people in certain ways to get the desired results, even if we have to treat them differently from one time to another. We do certain things because we get certain reactions; and because we can predict reactions to treatments, we change the treatment when we want a different reaction. Though this may sound like we become fickle supervisors, in reality we become skillful at knowing our people and how they will react under various conditions. We use the knowledge to get whatever results we desire. While this smacks of "manipulation," it's no more so than in any other kind of dealing with people. It's not unlike a parent-child, husband-wife, or friend-friend relationship. We just naturally deal with people in the best way we know how, realizing that knowing how they will react is part of human relationships. Knowing why people act the way they do is common knowledge at almost any age, even to children. While still in the crib, children learn that if they make certain loud noises and rattle the crib, they'll get certain reactions from their parents every time. (It may well be that even at this early age they're on their way to learning how to be supervisors!)

WHAT IS A STYLE?

Supervisory styles are varied, but simply put, a supervisory style is the way a supervisor goes about dealing with people in the day-to-day job. Styles are different kinds of behaviors we use to produce the reactions we need to get the job done. If you have an "autocratic" style, it means that you have the philosophy that bosses give orders and subordinates execute them without participating in the decisions and becoming involved in the job activity, so that orders need not be given every time something is to be done. If you have a "permissive" style, you think that subordinates should be allowed to determine their own actions without much supervision. If the employees don't want to do something, their supervisor should not force them. In the "participative" style, the idea is to let the employees participate in some or all of the decision-making processes and suggest how the job might best be done. They would be allowed to express themselves without fear of being chastised for it. The list goes on, and we'll see more about different kinds of styles later on. For now, we should point out that the best supervisors realize that flexibility requires that they have access to different styles and that they try to avoid settling on just one style for everyone in every situation. When the situation is right, they may become very permissive, whereas they may become autocratic at another time in another situation. As we'll see later, there are some dangers in this, but there are likewise dangers in keeping the same style under every condition with all different kinds of people. To maintain a flexible style, it is necessary to be a good judge of people and of the situation they are in. This brings us back to where we started: What do we know for sure about people? Let's see.

PEOPLE WANT TO BE TREATED FAIRLY OR BETTER

"Fairness" is a nice word with a good sound to it, but trying to determine in any situation just what is and isn't fair is a task that will create ulcers in even the wisest people. When it comes down to the final state of determining what is fair, we find that most often fairness is in the eye of the beholder. The situation has to be interpreted in terms of the person on the receiving end of the action. That person looks around, sees what is being done, and translates it into what it seems to mean in light of his or her attitudes, expectations, hopes, hang-ups, and so on. As we'll see later in this chapter, the interpretation usually will be based on a little *logic*.

Notice we've said that people want "fair or better" treatment. This means that they won't tolerate anyone else getting better treatment than themselves, but they won't necessarily object if they themselves come out a little better than fairness would have dictated. One simple example from everyday life will illustrate the point. If you leave your car parked by a meter overtime, fairness says that you should get an overtime ticket, especially if everyone else gets one for the same violation. However, if you arrive as the enforcement officer is beginning to write the ticket and talk him or her out of writing it, you are happy that you *weren't* treated fairly. You got better than fair treatment, and you were pleased with the outcome. You wouldn't have been nearly so pleased with just fair treatment! On the job, the same rule applies. If a certain infraction in a work rule carries certain discipline, the employees are less happy with the fairness of enforcing the policy than they are with getting better than fairness.

How does all this work out when we're talking about everyday supervisory activity? We find out that there is a lot of hypocrisy in supervisory ranks, although most supervisors wouldn't realize it unless they were shown the things they are doing. Perhaps the biggest problem supervisors have with hypocrisy is their inability to treat all their employees the same way because of *attitude* roadblocks. Employees with bad attitudes about some things may find that their supervisors treat them unfairly in all areas, whereas employees with good attitudes may get better treatment for the same actions as those with bad attitudes.

How supervisors feel about employees affects their treatment of them, even if the result is unfairness. That has sometimes been seen as hypocritical by those who hear them say, "Everyone has an equal chance around here." Fairness means giving every employee the same treatment for the same action. Perhaps this can best be seen in the following conversation, all too typical with supervisors. The two supervsors, Alice and Fred, are in the hall returning from the cafeteria. They both supervise work groups similar in duties and both have spent about the same length of time with the organization. Alice was hired as a supervisor and Fred worked his way up through the ranks. Each is considered a satisfactory supervisor, though they don't seem to develop all their people very well. Occasionally each will have a "star" performer who seems to be head and shoulders above the others in the group, but rarely will there be more than one in the group. Let's see if their conversation will reveal why that's so.

Fred: It was the same old thing. I told her to finish or forget it, and she got hot about it. She's given me trouble ever since she started with me. Some people are like that, though.

Alice: I'll say! I thought I'd fire one of my people this morning. I get so tired of telling my people the same old thing every day, especially when they have the kind of attitude Bob has.

Fred: Is that the guy you were talking about Friday? The one with the long curls? You ought to like him—he's got hair the same color as yours. 'Course, it's a little longer than yours!

Alice: Oh, I don't guess I mind the hair so much. It's just

that he has such an "I-don't-care" attitude. He just looks like he doesn't care whether he comes to work or not. I think it's a waste of time to hire people like that. There's no way he's going to stay here to have any kind of career.

Fred: You mean you're going to run him off?

Alice: No, that's not fair. I give him a chance, whenever he asks for it. I don't go out of my way to train him or show him anything, but if he'll straighten his attitude up, I'll give him some of my time. Gladly, too.

Fred: That's the point I was making about Doris a while ago. She messes around, makes errors, and then complains because I give the others more training than she gets. This morning took the cake. I just wish they all had the kind of attitude Wally has.

Alice: Which one is he? The one you said has never complained since he came to work for you? Some kind of miracle man, I'd say!

Fred: Yeah, I wish there were more miracles around. He may not be the best, but he can have my time anytime he asks for it. Even when he doesn't ask for it, as far as I'm concerned.

Alice: That's the way I felt about Mary when she was with me. Bless her heart, she'd try anything. She had a lot of shortcomings, and I guess I've had a lot of people who were more gifted than she, but I've never had one who had a better attitude. Some of the people resented my spending so much time with her, but it was always a pleasure to be around her. Don't know why the others resented her as much as they did. When I recommended her for promotion over some of the others, I thought some of them were going to quit, and they still mouth off about it every once in awhile.

Let's stop here and see what we've heard. What's the problem? Can't we all see the point Fred and Alice are trying to make? If you were to ask either of them if they were being unfair to any of their employees, they would be shocked at the thought. As we listen to them talking about Bob's long hair, we may think that there is some prejudice there; maybe this does have some influence on Alice's behavior, even though she didn't give it much emphasis. She did deal directly with our problem of the new work force, though, when she said she didn't like what she called Bob's "I-don't-care" attitude. When we look closely, however, we see that what she actually said was, "He just *looks like* he doesn't care whether he comes to work or not." Bob may be representative of the employees who will give older supervisors trouble if they judge people by their looks and their *apparent* attitude. Because of his looks, and maybe other things she didn't mention, Alice has decided that Bob isn't a career employee with this organization. Even if this were true—and surely even Alice wouldn't admit to knowing that for certain—as long as Bob is with her, he *always* deserves a chance to be trained. An untrained employee is an employee who isn't performing up to standard. It is conceivable that we could somehow justify the unfairness to the employee of not training him or her, but from the organization's standpoint there's no way we could justify keeping an employee untrained.

Notice Alice's concession to "fairness." She recognizes that "running Bob off" would be unfair, so she says she'll give him a chance *if he'll ask for it.* She puts the burden of responsibility on his shoulders, not hers, and makes it clear that she isn't going out of her way to train him or show him anything. However, if he'll straighten up his attitude, she'll give him some of her time. As we look at the newer workers and consider that they've been used to people giving them time, we'll realize that it's going to be hard for Bob to understand why he has to do something special just to be trained for his job. He'll see the inequity and the injustice, especially if his looks don't represent his attitude. The bad part about it is that he may not even have a bad attitude, or his attitude may be the result of instances when he missed the training he needed to perform up to the expectations of the organization that *wouldn't train him*. To add to the problem, he sees others being trained and doesn't know that the supervisor has put conditions on the training. We can be pretty certain that Alice hasn't revealed this to Bob, yet she goes around giving time to the other employees but not to him. What is he to think? There's a very good chance that he will interpret it to mean that she *does* resent the length of his hair, because during his formative years he's been conditioned to think that anyone older than he is will resent it.

Fred has exactly the same viewpoints concerning his employees as Alice does. Note that when Doris "messes around" and makes errors, she is ruled out of the training effort. He knows she needs training but gives it to the others because they aren't messing around. She *wants* the training, too, and that makes it doubly sad. She recognizes that others are getting training that she needs, and she is bound to see the unfairness in it all. Fred would justify his actions and see no unfairness in any of this. He points out in the very beginning that Doris has been giving him trouble since she came, but he's taken no action except to keep some of the training from her. It's his way of getting even with her for not having a good attitude like Wally, the apparent wonder. Interestingly enough, Wally isn't the best, but he can have all the time he wants. How fair is that? It isn't fair at all, but it seems to make sense to Fred and Alice, since they have decided that the employees have the first responsibility to "act right" before they get treated right. That's exactly the kind of hypocrisy the new workers have been aware of for a long time. The fact that fairness is in the eye of the beholder is best demonstrated by Alice's treatment of Mary. Note Mary's qualifications: she had a lot of shortcomings and less talent than others, but she was willing to try anything. She had a good attitude, so Alice spent more than an average amount of time with her, giving her training that finally provided her a chance to be promoted over those who were more talented but had less training. The organization lost the use of the more talented people and ended up with disgruntled employees who weren't permitted to advance as far as they were able because Alice based her decisions to train on attitude, not on potential. And who will say that this is a rare exception in today's work world?

Firmness with Understanding

One of the characteristics of people down through the ages is that they respect firmness in their leaders. In the sense that the supervisor is a leader, the subordinates will, in the long run, respect supervisors who are firm. "Firm" doesn't mean "hard as nails," and it isn't true that supervisors who are firm never smile, never give an inch on anything, and keep the employees in fear all the time. Rather, they consider the situation, the problem, and the alternatives, and make a firm decision that shows clearly that the decisions aren't up for vote.

The idea of firmness must also be associated with *fairness*. The idea of being firm takes on a new dimension when combined with the effort of trying to be fair as far as possible. New supervisors often have a problem handling both these elements at the same time, many times seeing a conflict between them. They think that words like "fair," "understanding," and "empathy" rule out firmness. Perhaps an ideal supervisor—given other necessary qualities—has an equal amount of firmness and fairness, seeing them as companions rather than as alternatives. Many new supervisors have made their own way difficult for a long time because they wanted so much to be liked that they combined their idea of fairness with "going easy" on the employees. The best advice to a new supervisor is to remember that in the long run *it's a lot easier to go from being firm to being easy than it is to go from being easy to being firm.* After a supervisor has gained the reputation of not being strict when he or she sets a standard, it's an uphill climb to change that reputation into a reputation for being firm and being serious about giving an order and getting the standard of expectation for that order.

The new workers will have some adjustments to make with regard to firmness, as it's a new experience for many of them. They aren't necessarily undisciplined, but they have just never had much exposure to firmness. For the most part, they haven't needed much of it because they have lived in a world that was rather permissive (especially at home and school), and they have maintained a degree of restrained behavior. This behavior came about as a result of thinking things through and deciding what was right and wrong. Since their behavior was often left to them to control, they have learned to exercise a measure of control that is probably less strict than the older supervisors would like, but fairly moderate by their own standards. There is, however, an almost inevitable conflict when supervisors begin to lean on this group, because the workers see their constraint as sufficient while the supervisors don't. The employees will need to make some adjustments in their lives and in their values, and this is always difficult and time-consuming. It can be done, but it will require that the supervisors be patient. *The wait is well worth the result.* This is the time to exercise *gentle* firmness rather than loud, haughty, and "lording-over-it" firmness. Try simple statements of expectations and directions and training as required, then let the employees alone. If the work isn't done properly, firmness requires that the prestated consequences be carried out straightforwardly, quietly, and immediately without emotion. Evidence has shown over and over again that this kind of treatment gets better results for a longer time than anything else we can do. There's no mystery to this; people respect us when we say something and keep our word, which in this case would be carrying out the steps outlined when we gave the employee the assignment in the first place. Keeping our word shouldn't be an "I told you so" or anything vindictive, and we should never make excuses for keeping our word!

Later we'll talk about "progressive discipline," but for now let's just say that firmness with fairness results in a kind of discipline that starts when the employee is told what the job requires and what the consequences are for violating specified rules. When the work rules are violated in some way, the employee is usually told again what the requirements are and that the next violation will result in certain kinds of action. On the next violation, this action is taken just as specified, and the employee is told that more serious discipline will come with the next violation. With each violation, then, the supervisor not only carries out the stated discipline but also states what is expected, encouraging the employee to think about doing the job correctly and reminding him or her what to expect if there is another violation. All this is obviously fair, and if done correctly, quite firm. There can be no complaint if there is discipline, since it has been specified ahead of time; the system breaks down only if the discipline is *not* carried out as stated. When it isn't, everyone recognizes that there has been a breach in the verbal "contract," and the supervisor will have a hard time with future enforcement.

Let's say a few words about "understanding." Since employees like firmness with understanding, we need to know just what "understanding" is. We often hear the word "empathy" used when we're talking about understanding. To understand someone fully, we need a degree of empathy to help us see how the other person feels, but the problem with empathy is that it often gets confused with "sympathy." Sympathy implies a certain amount of feeling about the person and the person's actions, and it even suggests that because we're sympathetic toward the person we might overlook certain actions. In reality, empathy is quite different; it tells us *why* a person behaves the way he or she does but leaves out any feeling or desire to overlook wrong behavior. From empathy we gain a knowledge of how people react to different kinds of treatment, so we have only to pick the results we want and then get them by using the kind of treatment that will produce those results. This doesn't mean that we don't have sympathy or feeling; it does mean that our decision about whether to be sympathetic depends on whether we think the situation deserves sympathy. If we have developed the necessary perception and sensitivity required to understand people, we employ the useful tool of empathy before action, not after it, choosing our action from the way we understand people. Sympathy is usually a reaction to something that has already happened.

We have to be careful that we don't let the fact that we know why a person did something interfere with our judgment. We may know that some people are habitually late and learn to expect them not to come in on time. We *understand* their problem and may even be sympathetic with some of the conditions that cause them to be late all the time, but we can't let this understanding keep us from dealing with the tardiness. Again, it's a matter of fairness. Even if we understand why people act the way they do, fairness calls for us to treat them just the same as we do anyone else, *including those whom we don't understand.*

PEOPLE WANT TO KNOW WHERE THEY STAND

One thing that has never changed about people is their desire to know where they stand in any situation. Workers have always needed to know this, and the younger workers are no different. Because they have been reared in a rather frank environment, their need to know how they are doing may be even greater than that of others before them. This is certainly true if they aren't living up to the standards, and they will resent it if they find out that we knew all along that they weren't performing but waited until appraisal time to tell them. We have to understand, of course, that they might not agree with our evaluation; if they don't, they'll most likely tell us. If we aren't used to employees being frank with and disagreeing with us, we may think they are being insubordinate; however, we should realize they are used to dealing with people frankly and will expect us to act the same with them.

Notice that this matter of wanting to know where they stand ties in with the earlier statements about firmness and fairness. If we think our people aren't doing as well as they should, fairness requires that we tell them about it. We must tell them what we expect of them, what they're doing that doesn't reach this standard, and what they can do to get up to standard. If we dread telling people they aren't performing well, then in a sense we dread being fair with people. Perhaps another word should be added to our list: firmness, fairness and *frankness.* If we can ever come to realize that people not only *want* to know where they stand but also *must* know in order to make whatever corrections are needed, we'll be more likely to tell them as soon as we have a good evaluation of their performance. The positive side of this is even more true, though it is often overlooked. People need to know the good things about their performance, too, and if we see that people are doing well and that they're performing up to or better than standard, then we're missing a good motivational opportunity if we don't tell them. Positive supervision is telling people how well they're doing, not just waiting until they foul up. Too many supervisors are afraid to tell their people when they perform well, fearing that the praise will cause them to slow down or to try to live on their merit. Yet all the studies about the subject say that *just the opposite is true.*

One of the reasons we can't always tell people how they stand is that we don't have a very good appraisal system. Any system we have should allow us to talk with the employees about their performance at reasonable intervals and must operate over a period of time to be fair. Things must follow a certain order and the sequence always begins with *telling the employees what standard is expected* of them on the job they're assigned to. Once they know what is expected, they must then be given the training to enable them to do the job and the time to show what they can do. It is at this point that the appraisal period really starts. The employees know what is expected, and they have been properly trained. We watch them along the way, making certain we've done a good job of training; when we see deficiencies, we step in and help them more, telling them what they're doing wrong *and* what they're doing right. As they grow, we offer encouragement and give them advice on ways to improve. We don't keep secrets from them but tell them *at the time* if we see them failing to meet the standards. At the end of the specified appraisal period, we have a frank discussion with them, reviewing their work over the whole period and talking about *both the good and the bad.* The key to this, though, is to avoid surprises at appraisal time. The actual appraisal should deal with things that have been discussed along the way, and it should be a planning session that looks ahead to the following year. If we spring a poor rating on an employee, we haven't done our job very well during the appraisal period. The appraisal is all part of the *firmness, fairness,* and *frankness* pattern of positive supervision.

PEOPLE RESPOND TO POSITIVE TREATMENT

It is no secret that people like to be rewarded for things they have done well. In fact, in almost every case people will be likely to repeat things for which they are rewarded, and it is equally true that they are likely to stop doing things that end in some kind of unpleasant experience for them. However, there is neither reward nor "punishment" for the vast amount of work we get from most people, and in this case they usually just level off to what is comfortable and habitual. They do their job and nothing happens—no feedback of any sort. We assume they understand that since we didn't chastise them in any way, they must have been doing a satisfactory job; as it turns out, that's a pretty good observation. This means that we shouldn't expect them to become overly motivated by the job when we fail to point out how they're doing; however, if we do praise a certain part of the work, they are likely to be more conscious of this than anything else, even letting part of their work slide to make sure they do well with the part we've praised.

What does this mean to a supervisor? Do we go around telling our employees how well they're doing every time they perform any job at all? Obviously we can't, and it certainly wouldn't prove very effective if we did. We should be selective with our praise just as with our constructive criticism. It is effective to watch for signs of employees performing quite well in a given situation, especially one in which they've not done too well in the past, and to step in to pass out words of praise. It doesn't have to be a sounding of the trumpet or a formal banquet in honor of the well-performing employee. It may be no more than a pat on the shoulder with the statement, "I liked the way you handled that!" We usually say that we "praise in public and correct in private," but even this isn't always necessary. In a routine job, if the employee knows we are watching, that's often all that's needed, though there may be a time to praise the employee in public if the job is done exceptionally well and if it will cause others to aspire to that same level of performance.

One of the biggest problems supervisors have in the matter of handing out praise is knowing how much to give and how often. To handle this correctly, we need to understand some things about people. Much of the answer to this problem depends on the workers' past history. If we're talking to a person who has experienced a great deal of success over the years and who faces every job with confidence, we don't get much out of a few words of praise about a routine job that wasn't really a very big challenge. On the other hand, if we're talking to an employee who has never experienced much success in any kind of work, even a small reward or word of praise for a job well done is exciting and *very* rewarding. If we understand our people well enough, we'll know what is needed in the way of

"I don't understand it. I just told them all they were doing a great job and still they goof off."

praise and reward. The rule of thumb is basically that those who have experienced frequent successes need fewer but larger rewards. For employees who have seldom seen success and who find a challenge in every job, no matter how small or insignificant, we offer smaller, more frequent rewards. Further, the *kind* of praise may differ with these two extremes. For employees who have experienced frequent success, we should praise them for accomplishing something challenging, which others probably would not have managed. The praise may be something like, "Hey, you've done that in record time! Don't see how you did it!" For the less successful employee, a comment on the performance will usually suffice. For example, "You've got that exactly right. I like that!"

PEOPLE WANT TO CONTRIBUTE

Everything we know about people in any work situation says that after all the smoke clears about money, time worked, working conditions, and benefits, people want to think that what they do is something *worthwhile.* There have been many examples in which workers apparently showed little interest in their jobs, "bad-mouthed" the organization, and appeared to have a very bad attitude about the work, the supervision, and the organization, but also demonstrated in some way that they were proud of their jobs. For example, let's say that on a worker's off day the organization has an open house and invites the families to come in to see the entire plant, setting a route for them to follow around the operation. Repeatedly we see employees ignoring the planned routing and taking their families directly to their work station; as they explain their part of the work operation, it sounds as if everything and everybody else were secondary in importance to them and their particular operation.

Over the years an idea called work simplification has worked against helping employees feel significant. In a later chapter, when we talk about motivation, we'll see the real damage this program has done to the efforts of supervisors in helping their employees feel needed. For now, though, we'll talk about some of the significance of work simplification.

The unfortunate thing about simplifying work into small portions is that much of the work is oversimplified to the point where *it really isn't very important.* To make that worse, even jobs that do have significance become hidden among the meaningless jobs, which frequently makes the workers feel unimportant even when they really have key jobs. Let's see how this happens.

First, in most simplification efforts, the work is divided among many different workers; each does only a portion of the job. Though many may be handling the same small operation, they have little or no communication with workers doing different jobs that are part of the same total operation. Each person sees himself or herself doing a small, routine task, with someone else on each side doing exactly the same task. For the most part, the job is so small that the employee needs to make no decisions, and the only measure of success is how fast and how accurate the job is done. While some people like this kind of work, workers who like variety and challenge are frustrated quickly. The newer members of the work force, who see themselves as able to contribute almost immediately, are quick to resist such assignments for any prolonged period.

Next, work simplification keeps employees from seeing the job from beginning to end. Things come to them, they perform some small operation, and then they pass the things on to somebody else. Few workers know where their work comes from or where it goes when it leaves them; it is impossible for them to feel a part of the total production as long as this is the case. Some wonder enough to ask questions; others just think that they'e stuck in a boring job with no hope of improvement.

Another reason why the employees do not realize when they have a significant job is that they never have what seems to be a total responsibility for anything. They have some responsibility for a small operation, but it doesn't feel like much responsibility when they don't see where things come from or where they go. While the responsibility they have may be quite significant to product quality or may even affect total production in some major way, they don't see enough to get the *feeling* of their responsibility. Unless their supervisors do a good job of explaining the significance, they'll feel they lack enough responsibility for the job to be very important.

Finally, all this works to make the individual feel totally insignificant and lost. The employee feels like part of a big machine, and in many ways he or she is just like another part of the machinery. Workers are programmed to work in ways similar to the equipment, are measured in output terms like the equipment, and sometimes are even replaced when they get old—just like equipment. Thinking about motivating people in situations like this certainly comes closer to being a nightmare than a dream!

What is the solution? Do we do away with the work simplification process? Few supervisors have that decision to make. We'll go into much more detail about motivation in a later chapter, but here we can look at a few things that the supervisor can do to help the situation.

Let's note again that the labor force coming into the work world now will find some tremendous problems in doing apparently meaningless tasks. Nearly everything that has happened to them up until now has been designed to let them fulfill their potential, feel important, and generally avoid dull, routine work. They will have a very difficult time adjusting to anything as dull and meaningless as some of the jobs available to them today. To make it worse, many older supervisors tend to forget what things were like when they were doing the hourly jobs, forgetting that they were working when the jobs hadn't been fragmented as much as they are today. All they remember is that they didn't complain as much about the job as today's workers tend to do. Ironically, even though they had more responsibility, they see the new workers as unable to take much responsibility and hence will not give them any. This, of course, adds to the frustration. It is similar to what we said about training: "Show you deserve it and you can have some!" It may be that the very absence of responsibility may make the employees appear uninterested and therefore unqualified for responsibility.

In addition to letting the workers' families see the entire operation, open houses are also very good for letting the *workers themselves* get a feel for the entire work function, as well as a feeling of importance. Various publications that are sent to employees' homes can accomplish the same thing, especially if they contain pictures, notices of awards, and explanations of the significance of various jobs. Whether we work in a plant or in an office, the idea is to let the employee see that the work is meaningful, especially through the eyes of family members or the community. This can be done by news stories, plant or office tours or open houses, or just simple house publications that go to the homes.

Another method that is easy yet effective is to hold meetings at which presentations are made to educate the employees about various departmental activities. These can be handled by the first line of supervision and are quite effective in spreading the knowledge of job significance.

These meetings are usually short, simply but well prepared, and delivered without any sales pitch or attempts at
brainwashing. The purpose is not to buy loyalty or overcome union strengths, but to let employees see that they
are a part of a bigger operation and that their part is important to that operation.

Another way to increase the employees' feelings about
their significance to the organization and to let them see
more of the tasks done by the different people is to do
some "cross-breeding." People from one operation move
to another part of the operation, seeing what the others are
doing and doing it themselves. Though the move may be
permanent or temporary, it can be called a training
program—as indeed it is—or it can be viewed as simply a
protective method for the organization, whereby some employees will have experience in several jobs. Frequently,
the employee who is involved in the move gets a good education on how his or her job fits in to the scheme of things
and spreads the word to those who didn't get moved.

One final way of publicizing the importance of each job
is to have a team handle the entire work operation, with
each member learning all the parts of the total job. Sometimes the supervisor does not have the authority to decide
this, but it works well when it is tried. Everybody learns everybody else's job, sometimes with no specific assignment, only a total job to be done with everybody trained to
do all the operations. This takes some good training effort,
but it gives the supervisor and the workers a great deal of
flexibility and knowledge about the job. Of course, this approach involves some problems, one being that when a replacement is necessary, the incoming employee has a
hard time becoming a part of the team and may feel left out
for a while. Also, each addition requires training for all the
operations, which can be rather time consuming. The training can be left to the rest of the team, but this requires

some follow-up to make sure the team has handled it adequately.

This discussion should not be closed without adding that perhaps the one thing that will have the most impact is for us to *believe in the importance of our employees and their jobs.* If we don't, we'll never convince them. We must get to know the employees, understand that they *aren't* machines, and remember that, just like us, they have feelings, concerns, plans, problems, families, money shortages, and personal conflicts and hang-ups. Because they are human beings they are important, and because they work for us they are even more important to us, no matter who they are or what they do. While no one of them is doing the total job, all of them together are. Any one of them has the potential of contributing to the success or failure of the whole performance of our section, group, or department. Most important of all, *they need to hear all this from us.* In telling them, maybe we'll come to believe it even more ourselves.

PEOPLE CARE ABOUT STATUS AND RECOGNITION

Although most people don't give it much thought, all organizations are full of status symbols. They range from valuable, tangible things to seemingly insignificant, psychological matters. To understand and recognize status symbols, we must first comprehend what status is and what makes it valuable. To have status, a thing must meet two criteria: It must be *considered* something to be wanted, and it must be something few people have. Its desirability decreases as more people have it; if people don't want it, its value is very low regardless of how many or how few have it. Almost everyone can find numerous examples within his or her own work group. When few people have their own desk, having one indicates status. When everybody has a desk, a desk is a must, but *it's not a status symbol.* If everyone has a metal desk and someone gets a mahogany desk, the wooden desk may become a status symbol even though it costs less or isn't as functional. The desk's location may also take on value. If a seat by the window, in the back, or near the front is deemed special, the person who has a desk there has status.

If everyone has an electric typewriter, a new person who gets one isn't getting much status. Suppose the organization has used only manual typewriters but has decided that from now on it will purchase only electric ones. In comes a new employee, with less experience and time with the organization than anyone else, and he or she is given the only electric typewriter in the office. To say that nobody would even notice is to think that cannonballs don't make holes in paper bags.

Status may come from being the only one in the shop to have personal tools. Perhaps everyone may have to check tools out except for one person—for whatever reason—who has a set to wear. We can be fairly certain that the person will be wearing them in the cafeteria, on break, in the parking lot, and maybe to bed! He or she has status and is making the most of it. On the other hand, if an edict comes down from management that everyone will be expected to carry his or her own tools, then everyone will grumble. When everybody *has* to carry them, what was once status becomes a drudgery.

While having one's own desk, chair, water pitcher, filing cabinet, private office, pictures on the wall, vehicle to drive, etc., may indicate status, intangible things can also be status symbols. People can *see* a desk or a name plate on the wall, and such things often become instant symbols because they are tangible items that represent power, prestige, or recognition. The person who doesn't have them sees them and wishes for them, increasing the desire and the degree of status. But some intangible status symbols are equally desirable. For example, when the boss says to an employee, "From now on I'll direct people to you when they have a question about this," he or she has just passed out some status. One person's selection to answer questions about some part of the operation is a distinction that others don't have. Since answering questions, and *being recognized as the answerer,* is a form of prestige, employees who may not even be able to answer the questions may envy the assignment. It may be a chore for the person doing it, disrupting normal routines and involving dealings with unpleasant people; however, because of the status involved, she or he keeps the assignment and guards it with a high degree of jealousy. When there is a change in the game plan and the boss says, "From now on everybody will be expected to answer any questions directed by people who want information on this," then it is no longer a status symbol to answer questions and no one is happy with the assignment. More examples could be given, but the point is clear. People like to have some status, and even though they may not admit it, we can find out in a hurry how much they like it by trying to take it away from them!

What does this mean to the supervisor? Do the new working people have the same feelings about status? The answer is that they do care about these things and will compete just as much as anyone else for the status, if it is available. Their idea of what is important may differ a little, but there's no evidence to indicate that they don't get satisfaction from wearing a select kind of uniform or having their own widget when nobody else is allowed to have one, or that they don't feel the same pangs of envy and desire when they see others with things they don't have. The only difference in them is that they may come right out and ask why they don't have it. They may be much more frank about it and expect a frank answer in return. We can use this desire for prestige by finding out what work the group considers important and making certain that we don't overuse it. We must make certain that we don't try to motivate everyone by giving it out in wholesale lots. We use the status sparingly and wisely, giving it only to deserving people, and we don't make a major production out of it, because the work group wll do that for us. We can even role-play innocence when we announce the awarding of a work assignment or some of the more tangible symbols, doing it because it is the natural thing to do, not a reward. However, we should do it only when we feel an award is in order.

EVERYBODY WANTS TO BE BETTER THAN SOMEBODY AT SOMETHING

All we have to do is stop and listen to people talking at lunch or over coffee or in the carpool to see that most of us want to impress others that we are better in some way. This starts way back in the sandpile. My truck is bigger and faster and will haul more sand than yours will. My father can lick your father; my mother is prettier than your mother; my brother is stronger than your brother. This is not really much different from desire for status except that we're trying to make our own. For example, when someone tells about a fishing trip, *his* fish was the biggest, took the longest to land, or was caught with his own secret lure, or (if all else fails to win him a top position) he fought the longest and wound up with the *smallest* fish of all. We like to have the best car, get the best mileage, use the least oil, or have tires that wear the longest. We carry this attitude right over to the job; we want to be better than somebody at something.

When we talk about a problem, we like to make it a kind of problem that nobody else ever had, and when somebody comes along and tries to solve it for us, we may even avoid the solution, since having the problem gives us a form of status. We like to avoid the solution with words like "Yes, but . . ." or "I know it sounds simple, but you don't understand. . . ." This is especially true if we've managed to get some attention out of the problem or if the solution begins to sound so simple that the size of the problem diminishes. Since we're all guilty of this at one time or another, it should be easy to spot other people who are having the same problem with their desire to outdo somebody else. One trouble with this is that, in our own subconscious way, we may resent hearing somebody "bragging" and thus try to put the person down. We may even react to our own need to excel and feel that they are taking something away from us. When we think about it, though, *using* this trait in people is better than trying to *overcome* it. Let's see how supervisors can use it to their advantage, especially when the employees are new to the work force.

New workers have very little that they can do or be that is better than someone else in the organization can do or be. Since many of those in the new generation have some frustrations, conscious or otherwise, in trying to "find themselves," they will feel this need for being better than others even more acutely than some of the older, more established workers. One reason they haven't "found themselves" is that in many ways they were so much a part of the herd of young people who grew up along with them that they were very "equal" to everybody else. In sports they were involved in things where everybody, not just the good ones, had a chance to play. They were a part of the movement for "equality" in every walk of life, and their need to be better than somebody at something often ended up being fulfilled only by feeling smarter than their parents. They decided that their parents and teachers "just aren't with it" and this meant they themselves were "with it" and hence better than somebody.

As their supervisors, we have an excellent opportunity to give them a chance to excel in real ways. There are some cautions, though. First, we must be careful not to play games with them. We shouldn't tell them they're doing something well just to build them up if they really aren't doing any better than anyone else. We must also remember that even though the more experienced employees may have their need to excel filled more easily, they still have the need. If we start taking away from them to give recognition to the newer employees, we'll have a hard time satisfying the older group, too.

How does it work? Knowing that the newer employees need to see themselves as being better than somebody at something, *we play them against themselves.* If they're learning a new job, they'll have some problems at first, making some errors, being slow, and failing to make the quotas set for them. After a while, though, they'll start to improve, often very dramatically. It is at this point that we can step in and show them that they've learned very well in a short time. We might say, "I can't believe how much you've improved over the last week," or "In less than a month on the job you've gone from 40 percent of quota to 74 percent of quota!" Note that while these statements represent solid praise and give them a chance to be better than themselves and *imagine* that they might be learning faster than others have in the same time, we haven't in any way at all put the older workers to shame. We aren't saying that the newer employees are better than the older ones. It's obvious that at most they're only approaching *standard,* whereas the experienced workers are meeting the standard all the time, perhaps even exceeding it most of the time. Whatever we do to make an employee feel superior, *we shouldn't do it at the expense of another employee.* In virtually no cases can we ever accomplish anything constructive within a work group by showing that one employee is doing better than another. The exception to this may be in sales. Building one employee up by comparing him or her with another simply tears down the other employee, leaving things in worse shape than before.

CONCLUSION

Although people may differ, depending on their background, experience, and time of rearing, they also have many things in common. In fact, people have some common traits that make it possible to predict certain results from certain kinds of treatment. We've looked at some of the more significant characteristics of people of all ages, not exhausting the list but seeing ways to use some of the more obvious ones. We've seen, too, that even though the new working people are different in many of their value systems, it is fortunate for supervisors that they are very similar in important ways to all the people who have worked over the years. We started out talking about developing a "style" of supervision and ended up realizing that the solution lies in understanding people and in using that information in dealings with them. The good supervisors are the ones who have learned enough about people to predict their behavior under certain conditions. They've learned that most people are alike in many ways and that getting a particular result frequently requires supervising in a particular way. In other words, certain actions produce certain reactions. Although this may be somewhat oversimplified, it's not so far from accurate that we can't use the principle to learn to supervise successfully.

What do we know for sure about people? We have quite a lot of usable information:

1. People want to be treated fairly (or better).
2. People want firmness with understanding.
3. People want to know where they stand.
4. People respond to positive treatment.
5. People want to contribute.
6. People care about status and recognition.
7. People want to be better than somebody at something.

That's a pretty impressive list, even though it covers only some of the important characteristics. There are more, and as we go through this book we'll look at them as they fit into the subject matter being discussed. Note that this is information that can be used, not just theories and intangible things that a supervisor can't apply on the job. The fortunate thing is that the information can be applied to the work force at any level and in any age group; we can test them, because *they apply even to us!* As we think about developing a style we should use with certain kinds of people, we would do well to look at the preceding list and ask what kind of style will use this information. We haven't suggested any specific style—and won't for the reasons already mentioned—but we can say that a style that will give us difficulty is one that treats everybody alike all the time under all situations. Some will try to call that "consistency," but it turns out to be *inflexibility*. As we develop empathy and get to know people better, we'll have many different *actions* for different *people* at different *times* under different *circumstances*. The one thing we can say about developing a style that should fit every supervisor is that whatever style we use and whatever action we take *should have a reason behind it*. We do things because we know fairly well what to expect as a result of doing them. If we don't get the results we expected, then we analyze the actions and decide what happened and what we can do differently next time to get the desired results. Supervision is a "thinking" activity. We can't just react without thinking and expect to get good results all the time. We may be successful sometimes, but the other times can be disastrous, and we won't like it when that happens. That's something else we know for sure!

DISCUSSION QUESTIONS

1. What is a supervisory style? How important is it to be flexible in our style?

2. Make a list of things we know for sure about people.

3. How is it that fairness is in the eye of the beholder? Discuss the conversation between Fred and Alice in relation to this idea of fairness.

4. How has work simplification worked against helping employees feel significant?

5. What are some things we can do to increase the employee's feeling of self-worth and value to the organization?

6. How does status work in motivating people? What criteria must a thing meet to have status?

part three

Solving Problems
in Supervision

Chapter five

Problem Solving

No one will be successful until he or she learns the skill of problem solving. We must be able to deal with all kinds of problems that arise from many different sources and under many different kinds of conditions. When we read a statement like this, we are tempted to say, "So, everybody knows *that!*" But do we *really* know it? If we listen to supervisors talk, we might think that even if they did know it at one time, they have forgotten that problem solving is an integral part of their job. We often hear supervisors saying things like, "Supervision would be a lot easier if we could just get the right people for the job." Statements such as this are typical of many we are likely to hear in almost any organization. They say that *supervision is made difficult by problems.* What they are really saying is that if the organization would get a better policy for hiring, their job would be simpler. In other words, if the organization would just allow us to hire people with good attitudes and aptitudes, put them in the proper jobs, and then give the right kind of management support for using these people in their jobs, we wouldn't have so many problems. Further, if the organization would let us give the employees the necessary equipment and tools to do the job and give us enough space and furniture to get the work force organized properly, then make the communications lines flow so they could get the right information from the right people at the right time to use it, see to it that they get the needed support from the other work groups and give us enough authority to handle the job as it should be handled, we could do the job the way management wants it done.

There's just one small problem with all of that: If we had it, just why would we need supervisors anyway? If all the employees are just right for the job, if the jobs fit the employees, and if the employees have such good attitudes, then any problems would be few and far between and not very serious anyway. The kind of workers we would have could easily solve the problems themselves. While all this is mythical—no one will ever meet all those conditions—it makes a simple point. *We have supervisors because we have problems.* Supervisors are needed to solve these problems, taking the less-than-right people on jobs they don't exactly fit, putting them into situations where their attitude is not quite right, working them where the furniture, equipment, and space is less than totally suitable and management policies and support may be inadequate, and yet getting the job done satisfactorily. We may look around at our people, the jobs, and the organization and its policies and decide that there's no way the job can get done properly; however, in the face of this we have to admit that other supervisors *are* getting the job done under all the same conditions. Therefore we must do so, too.

THE NEED TO SOLVE PROBLEMS CORRECTLY

As we've concluded, we need to learn to solve problems. However, since problem solving for the most part is a skill, it must be learned because not many of us are born

Since there was some confusion about the meeting to discuss improving communications which was scheduled Tuesday, but postponed tentatively to Thursday depending upon the availability of the meeting room Wednesday, it has been decided to reschedule it for those who did not attend, depending upon a more convenient time. Let us hear from you soon unless you already have.

with the talent to do it perfectly. Even though we solve problems all the time and tend to think that we are good at it, we aren't doing it very well if we aren't going through the steps discussed in this chapter.

Interestingly enough, the steps in problem solving haven't changed much over the years, even though other supervisory skills have. People have changed in the kind of problems they cause, but the skills needed to solve them haven't. One thing we should notice about the new working people is that they are probably better equipped to do logical problem solving than almost any other generation. Because of the general permissiveness with which many of them grew up, they were allowed to deal with problems more freely and hence can look at situations with less prejudice or preconceived notions. As is always the problem with newer workers, though, they lack the experience gained from actually doing the job for awhile, which is something the older employees have in their favor. Many of the older workers, including older supervisors, bring their biases and inflexibility to their problem-solving efforts, resulting in solutions that are probably not very imaginative. Tradition will probably rule the thinking of most of these people, causing conflict between the older supervisors and the newer workers. The new generation is going to have a difficult time understanding some of the solutions, especially if the solutions ignore their own suggestions. It will get even more troublesome if the explanation of why it's being done a particular way is that "we've always done it this way." Problem solving is a skill, though, and it can be learned. In this chapter we'll try to see just what makes good problem solving.

WHAT IS A PROBLEM?

It may sound like an oversimplification, but in most organizations problems arise because somebody somewhere *hasn't done the job properly*. The problem may arise from poor planning, a lack of controlling, bad supervision, poor training, or maybe no training at all. It could come from a combination of many things. It might be from some failure that happened a long time ago or from something that has just happened. Whatever and wherever, somebody did something wrong and a problem now exists. But just what is a "problem"? It's a situation in which things don't go as they are *supposed* to go. We have a plan, expect something to happen, or believe that we know the situation and all the elements in it, but then, for some reason, things aren't like they're planned, expected, or supposed to be. In a way, a problem is an obstacle in the way of what would otherwise be a smooth, direct route from one known place to another. We have to stop and deal with the obstacle that wasn't a part of the original plan. We must take some other action just to get around the obstacle, spending more time, redirecting people's energy, and using additional, unplanned resources.

If we can accept that as a legitimate definition of a problem, then there are times when we have a problem and don't realize it. Now we have a measure to go by. We ask ourselves, "Am I spending more time with this employee than I had planned to?" If the answer is positive, then we may have a problem. We need to look at what we are doing with our time and energies and what we're worrying about the most. What do I spend my time talking about? When I'm on break, at lunch, or in the carpool, is there one thing that I keep complaining about or wishing I could get off my mind? Do I have uneasy feelings even though I'm not certain exactly why? As I walk through the office or plant, do I find myself checking on one thing more than anything else? Is there some situation that I keep defending more than I really should have to, saying things like, "I'm sure it will work out okay; just give it a little time"? Do errors keep coming from the same source? Is there an employee who exhibits a good attitude and whom I really like, but who is late or absent more than the rules allow or sometimes performing below average? Do I hate to say anything to him or her because I don't want to damage the good attitude? The answers to these questions will tell me better than anything else if I have a problem.

The same definition may tell us that we *don't* have a problem when we think we do; actually, this is harder to spot than the problem. Sometimes we do a lot of talking and thinking about things because we think we have a problem. We check on people even though their work is satisfactory every time we check; we fail to give someone an assignment because we think it might cause a problem, even if it's been a long time since that person caused us a problem. We overreact to normal situations because we *think* we're going to have a problem. We talk about problems, trying to get others concerned even when they don't see any problems. Because they see things going as they should, they aren't the least bit sympathetic with our worrying.

One reason many of us have had problems with the newer work force is that we spend a lot of time predicting the problems, and in some ways we even make these self-fulfilling prophecies. We measure the new workers by our standards of behavior, values, and attitudes, and automatically we expect them to be problems. From the very beginning of their employment we treat them as though they were problems, and it doesn't take long until this treatment makes them problems. Because we think they're going to have a bad attitude, we watch them closely to make sure they don't leave early, keep closer tabs on them than on other new employees in the past, and watch their performance the same way. We are watching their work more to catch them fouling up than to help them do a better job. We don't admit this to ourselves, but we will admit that we expect less from these employees than we do from others, or at least that we expect them to be *problems.* They come to us expecting to do a job, but we fail to give them responsibility, thinking that they are not very responsible. Getting no responsibility, they become disinterested. Then we say to ourselves, "See there! They really aren't interested in the job. They have a bad attitude. They are a problem!" They are, in fact, a problem now, but because we have made them that way.

Of course, the new work force isn't the only problem we have, and it isn't the only thing we read incorrectly when we are trying to decide whether we have a problem. It takes good judgment to know when we have a problem, and many of us aren't very good at it, either because we like the martyrdom of having problems or are too naive to recognize certain kinds of problems. Perhaps the most common fault we all have is that we never really stop to define what is or isn't a problem. We take things as they come, handling each situation as it arises, sometimes overreacting, or sometimes reacting either too slowly or too quickly. As we'll see later, knowing we have some kind of a problem is the first step, but being able to define the problem exactly is the next—and much harder—step.

HOW DO WE REACT TO PROBLEMS?

Perhaps the most natural reaction is *frustration*. We have a plan that we want to work so we can get on to something else. We have only a given amount of time and energy, and we'd like to see it used productively to reach a goal that either we or somebody else has set. Then along comes something that keeps us from reaching that goal as we'd planned. Perhaps it's something over which we had no control, such as a cut in the budget or the loss of an employee. Our first reaction is probably frustration. From that point on, it's a matter of how we handle frustration, rather than how we solve problems. We may shrug it off and go on solving the problem. We may run from the problem, trying to give it to somebody else or saying we've "had it" with trying to reach the goal. We may try to get somebody else to take it over, or we may just give it up as a lost cause. None of these is a very good way of handling frustration and isn't likely to get us far as supervisors. If we aren't careful, we can set up a pattern of reacting to frustration in this manner, and it will become not only natural but also habitual. It will be a difficult habit to break because we're saying to ourselves, "If I run I won't have to deal with this problem. If I don't run I'll have to face it, solve it, and deal with some unpleasantness." The alternative to running won't always appeal to us, but we have to learn to get our rewards from the results, not from the actions that got us the results.

Another reaction to problems is to look for *blame* instead of solutions. When things suddenly start to go all wrong, we may start to protect ourselves, immediately thinking of saving our own necks. This natural reaction can become a habit very quickly. Rather than trying to get out of the situation by solving the problem, we think of ways to place the blame on somebody besides ourselves. Even if we see we can't extricate ourselves from total blame, we at least try to get somebody else in the boat with us as it goes down. We need to think of how many times we hear somebody (ourselves) say, "Well, it's not *my* fault!" or, "I didn't have anything to do with *that* part of the work." Instead of protecting the organization by trying to solve the problem, regardless of whose fault it is, we jump in and try to protect ourselves, letting the organization come second. This is the kind of hypocrisy that the new work force learned to object to in their formative years. They hear us demand loyalty to the organization, then watch us let the organization go down the tubes when it looks like we might suffer. In such a situation they wonder about our loyalty, and perhaps they have a valid point!

Sometimes when we are faced with a problem, we just *plow right through,* refusing to vary from our planned path. This means that we end up "busting some heads," sometimes including our own. When an obstacle is in our way, we take it as a personal challenge and feel there is no way to go but straight at it. Some call it determination; some call it bullheadedness; some call it lack of problem-solving skill. We have to be careful in taking this approach, even though in some cases it might be the best. We simply have to ask ourselves if the victory is worth getting this way. Will plowing through use up too much energy, time, and resources, or are we saving them in the long run? If we don't consider the alternatives and still try to go right through because we don't like to vary once we've set our course, we can easily define our action as bullheadedness and poor problem-solving skill. However, if we look at the alternatives, make cost and time comparisons, and then decide that it's worth the discomfort and energy we'll have to expend, it's most likely determination.

We must be careful in using this approach because we may injure those who are helping on the project or who are a part of the action in some way. This is especially true if we begin to punish those who reveal facts we don't want to hear. When we jump on people for bringing us bad news about how things are going, we'll soon stop getting the bad news; however, not getting it doesn't mean it isn't still there. We may be sure that this is becoming a habit with us when we begin to enjoy having only those people around us who tell us that things are going along just fine. It's not so much that they are the "yes men" of older days, but that they just know we like to hear good news and tell us whenever they have some. When we ask about a project or ask if there's a problem, they work very hard at assuring us that things look all right. They may be judging from correct but incomplete information, they may know how much this particular project means to us and don't want to discourage us, or they may just be very optimistic people. Whatever the reason, if we reward only people who bring us good news and punish those who bring us bad, sooner or later things will begin to collapse around us. When they do, all those who were bringing only the good news will disappear, and the ones with the bad news will have every right to say, "I told you so!" Neither group will be much help to us at that time.

As we have said, we might sometimes succeed with the plow-right-through method. However, if we go beyond the point of profitable return, we have probably done the organization and our people damage instead of good. If we haven't considered the facts, our people will begin to lose confidence in us and question our ability to lead them. They, too, may become frustrated with the way things are going. The newer working people, who have always asked why and expected a reasonable answer about anything they were told to do, will be first to spot the lack of logic in this approach. If it becomes obvious to them that there is a better way or that our way doesn't make sense, then we compound the problem when we give no better reason than "Do it because I told you so." This approach can bring on some real rebellion from them. The end of all this is that we will lose our own effectiveness by wasting time, energy, or money on a goal that may not be worth it to the organization, while we could have been working on some other project.

Another way to react to problems is to search diligently for an *alternate goal*. We look at what we've accomplished so far toward the prescribed goal, then decide how we can make use of that effort in reaching a different goal. Often this means that we stop short of getting where we intended to go. Perhaps we've set a production goal but have discovered that certain things aren't going well enough for us to reach that goal. We then consider how much we lack and choose to settle for less production. *That's picking an alternate goal.* Suppose that we have an unsatisfactory employee who needs discipline, which we decide to administer without further delay. But as we look at our documentation we realize we haven't kept records that are as complete as the work agreement calls for. How do we react to this problem? We can just give up, saying that there's no way we can carry out good discipline and blaming it on the labor relations people, or we can go ahead in spite of the poor documentation, risking losing a grievance and costing the organization time and money. Perhaps we can come up with a lesser form of discipline, settling for a reprimand instead of a suspension. *That's picking an alternate goal.*

A final way to react to problems is to choose an alternate way of reaching the original goal. This should be our first approach. We have put enough time and thought into the original plan to make it worthwhile, so we should make certain before we leave it that that goal is no longer possible. As we've discussed before, this doesn't mean that we just plow right into the situation, but it does mean that we look at the obstacles and decide what it would take to reach the goal if we went some other way. Usually it involves using a little more time or money or more people, and it may require some brainstorming or imagination to think of something else we can do to get where we're going without giving up anything. The first move is to count the cost of continuing toward the same goal. In the case of the production goal mentioned earlier, we first decide what it would take to get the production level we want. Possibly all that's needed is some overtime. That will take money, but we can evaluate that and decide whether it's worth it. It may mean that we'll have to get advanced shipment for some of the raw materials, but, again, these things are measurable. We may need some statements from higher management in terms of how much money is available for overtime and just how much the production goal is worth to the organization. If we panic, give up, or just walk around and scream at our workers to work harder, we won't accomplish the goals; however, if we stop and do a little intelligent thinking, we can make some reasonable decisions about reaching the original goal in a different way.

Thinking about the discipline problem may still get us to the original goal of severe discipline. We can go back over the personnel records to see documentation from previous jobs or the other supervisors; we can look at the time factors to see if we want to continue gathering data instead of taking action. Time is the consideration, and two things could happen in that time. We might find that the employee's performance is so poor that it may damage production or the morale of others. Or we might find that her or his behavior will change for the better and that discipline won't be needed. Of course, this would be the best of all worlds, because we never want to take any action just to "catch" somebody so we can discipline her or him. We weigh the time, production, and morale factors, and then decide if the original goal is still the best one. If it is, then we've done a good job of facing our problems. Even if we decide to go some other route to another goal, we've at least tried to pursue the original goal until it became impractical.

A philosophical question needs to be dealt with here. This book has constantly suggested that supervisors take a positive appoach to the work laid out before them. Later in the book we'll talk about something called PMA (positive mental attitude). There are those who seem to dwell on the reasons why things can't be done, but a good supervisor always thinks of ways things *can* be done. Every problem should be faced not as an impossible obstacle but as part of the job. As we've seen, it's the supervisor's job to solve problems. Each obstacle is merely part of the job, but it is also somewhat of a test of how good someone is as a supervisor. Supervisors with a *positive* approach view the obstacles in a way that is different from supervisors with a negative approach. Supervisors who see everything as negative see an obstacle—a problem—and say, "We can't reach our goal because of this obstacle." Positive-minded supervisors see the same obstacle and say, "We can reach our goal by overcoming this obstacle." It is the same obstacle viewed in two different ways, positively and negatively. The chances of overcoming the obstacle with a negative approach aren't nearly as good as they are with the positive approach. *Supervisors won't get their job right until they get their minds right.*

GENERAL STEPS IN PROBLEM SOLVING

There are some steps in problem solving that every good supervisor follows. This isn't to imply that a supervisor sits down and names these steps each time a problem arises. There are those who would suggest this, but it's ridiculous to expect that each problem be attacked with such a formal approach. A busy supervisor will have many, many problems within any given day, sometimes even within the hour. If problems can be solved only by rattling off a list of "steps to problem solving" and then checking off each step as it has been done, few problems will get solved. However, we need to understand and go through some steps as we face problems. Ideally, we'll get in the habit of going through them, so we don't have to name each step. By reviewing them here, we can see that they are logical enough for us to start using them with the bigger problems and gradually work our habits to the point where we just naturally think in these terms.

Be Certain a Problem Exists

We've already dealt with this in much detail and have seen the ways of telling if we really do have a problem. We can locate it by seeing how much time and energy we spend "worrying" about it. The worst possible way a supervisor can spend time is by trying to solve nonexistent problems.

Be Certain to Solve the Real Problem

Although it has been said by many people, it bears repeating here. *We should always deal with the problem, not the symptom.* If we have a morale problem, we need to deal with whatever is causing the problem, instead of trying to make the employees happy by doing additional things for them. If we have an employee who is disinterested, we shouldn't try to improve the attitude but should deal with whatever is causing the disinterest, whether it be the job, the lack of responsibility, or the lack of training. It may even be poor supervision. Many organizations have introduced massive programs to deal with problems they see in an employee attitude survey, only to find that the problem was something else entirely. For example, organizations have instituted supervisory training programs when the real problem was lack of communication up and down the line of management. The training was enjoyable and perhaps did some good, but the real problem still exists since it wasn't dealt with.

Gather Enough Facts to Deal with the Problem

When we have decided that a problem exists and know what the problem is, the first impulse is to dive right in and solve it with the information at hand. A much safer approach, however, is to gather enough data to deal with the problem intelligently. We must admit to ourselves that we'll never get all the information we'd like to have, so we also have to know when to stop trying to get more. There is no ironclad rule of thumb on this, but one way to get a feel for it is to see if we have ideas and facts about several different sides of the issue. Do we have good solid data on several approaches to the matter that's causing the problem? If there is a constant lack of following directions and if we have defined the problem as one of a breakdown in our communications with our employees, we need to have examples of actual failures, some from people who failed to get the information, and examples of cases where we thought we were doing a good job but still failed. Do we have samples of information-giving documents? When we are pretty certain that we have gathered enough information to see both sides of the problem, we are ready to pursue the solution. If we have only one side or "our" side, we aren't ready yet. One final caution here: It's already been stated that we'll never have all the information we'd like, but there's a danger in letting this be an excuse to keep us from going ahead in dealing with the problem. We can hide a long time behind this excuse. When someone asks us if we've solved the problem yet, we can always say, with some legitimacy, "We're still gathering information so we won't overlook any possibilities." Good judgment will have to tell us when it's time to go to the next step.

Hold Off Solving the Problem as Long as Possible

This sounds like a contradiction of the last things we've been talking about, but it's really just a caution, not a full-fledged step. Once we have some information, our inclination is to jump to an immediate solution without looking for or considering enough alternatives. We need to do some analysis and synthesis (taking apart and rearranging) before we can get a clear picture of things that will help us overcome the problem. Each time we get another set of facts, we tend to jump to conclusions with an "I know what to do" statement. The rule here is to *keep an open mind as long as possible.* If we think about it, we'll realize that the first thing we decide to do when we have a problem is usually *not* what turns out to be the best, even though at the time it seems to be the obvious thing to do. Later, as we do more thinking with the facts we've gathered, we see that another solution is much more satisfactory.

Find Alternate Solutions

Whenever we're faced with a problem, often the first thing we do is pick the most obvious solution. We've just seen that with a little thought we may find that our first impulse may not be the best one, even though it may seem that way at first. Time is a good tester, and if we don't do anything else, we at least ought to meditate over the solution for a little while before choosing the first solution. (Some may ask at this point if we are suggesting that people can't make good decisions in a rapid way. But we're not talking about decision making right now; we're talking about problem solving in which there is a little more leeway in time. We have to make decisions during the problem-solving process, and it helps if we can make good decisions in a hurry. Usually people who make fast decisions can do so because they have had a lot of experience in the field in which the decisions are made or have developed skill by making and testing many decisions.) While we look at the obvious solution first, we need to avoid looking at only the obvious. We also have to avoid looking at only the *traditional* solution. When we decide on a solution, the first thing we ought to ask ourselves is whether we chose it because *it's the way we've always done it.* There's usually a good reason why we always do things the same way, most often because it is a time-tested and proven way. We can't knock things just because we've always done them that way, but there are some things that we do the same way all the time that haven't been challenged. By challenging them, we might find that they aren't all that good as a way of doing things. This means that we should take a hard look at at least two things before making a final decision: our first impulse and the traditional solution.

Where do we get alternate solutions? One way is to use a brainstorming process, in which we simply collect ideas without challenging them until we've run out of ideas. Nothing is considered too ridiculous because we know that we aren't going to use all the ideas anyway. By brainstorming, even to the point of being ridiculous, we will get some imaginative ideas, some of them usable. We can improve the brainstorming idea by getting several people in on the activity. It can even be done in a formal kind of way with someone keeping track of the ideas, maybe even recording them on an easel as they come up. The rule is that no one is allowed to object or be critical of an idea until the process of generating new ideas is completed. At that time—and this is after several silences, not just the first one—each idea is considered on its merit by talking about both its good and its bad aspects. Many ideas will be thrown out as too ridiculous or too impractical, but several will be accepted for further consideration.

The same people we call in to brainstorm with us can be used even without this formal process. We can simply ask them to give us their views on certain aspects of the problem because of their specific experience and expertise. When we have done this, we put them together to increase our base of knowledge, thereby giving us more insight into the alternatives we already have and allowing us to add some more. As we'll see later, we can test our ideas with these same people, but we should avoid testing ideas until we're certain we've got all the reasonable alternatives.

One final source of good ideas is the young work force, because they bring several skills and characteristics with them to the job that makes them good at finding good solutions to problems. First, they have good minds and have had some experience in dealing with challenging problems, if only because most of them have had more education than the workers before them had. Second, they aren't as steeped in tradition as older workers usually are, so they can look at the problem with fresh points of view. Perhaps the most important reason for going to these people for assistance in solving problems is that, for the most part, their confidence level is very high. Many of them don't know they can't do things and often end up doing them. They have the ability to look at things objectively, giving new approaches that are different from those of the older workers. Finally, they usually like the challenge of doing things in new and different ways and of solving difficult problems. We make a big mistake and miss a chance to add some motivation to their jobs if we don't let them participate in problem-solving opportunities like this.

Test Possible Solutions

Earlier we suggested that we ought to wait as long as possible to come to a solution because we need as many options as possible before we make a final decision. These options or alternatives need to be tested, though, because it is in this phase of problem solving that we will pick the solution. All the ideas need to be checked to see if they really are usable, and in order for all to get a fair hearing, we have to set some standards for testing these ideas. The criteria can be any number of things or combinations of several. Money, people, time, ease of application, availability of experience or material, or acceptability among the employees (or clients) may be used to help pick several of these and set some limits on each one. We can decide that the solution must not exceed a set amount of overtime, must cost no more than a certain amount, must have top management's approval, and must allow us to finish the work by a specified date. Once we've settled on the standard by which to test the ideas, we must use it in every case.

The pitfall we must avoid at this point is to allow ourselves to weed out possible solutions because of personal prejudice. The whole process we've been through up to this point falls apart if we come this far and let personal biases rule out an otherwise good idea. Once we've decided what we think is the best possible solution and are ready to go with it, we may need to try it out on somebody whose judgment we trust. At this point we don't need a devil's advocate, but somebody with good sense who will react only to the *possibility* that we'll use this as a solution. We don't try to justify it; we just ask the person, "What do you think of doing thus and so?" The only hazard we run into at this point is that if we ask a person who might have some very strong biases, we may get a negative answer and become disillusioned about the idea we've picked even though it passed the tests we gave it. We have to remember two things: we did go through a rather scientific process to come up with the solution we have; and second, the person we're talking to hasn't had the advantage of all our information or reasoning. Then why test it on someone at all? Simply to see how the idea hits somebody else. Sooner or later we have to present it to others, so we might as well get some reactions as soon as possible.

Once we've satisfied ourselves that we've got the best solution, we're ready for the next step. Ready, that is, if we're really confident that the idea is the best one. Before going on, it's always a good idea to document the idea so that if anyone comes up with any questions we can provide our thought processes, although about the worst thing we can do is present our whole problem-solving process for everyone to look at. If we've done our homework, we should have enough faith in the final choice to present it in such a way that it will stand alone. We can show that this solution is the way to go, but we don't have to show why all the others we considered aren't the best. This could take a lot of time and only add a great deal of confusion. If questions do arise about other choices, we should be able to deal with them, but usually it's best to leave the unused solutions alone until someone asks about them. Even at this point we should give only enough information to show that we did consider the idea and ruled it out in favor of the one we're presenting.

Plan the Action

There have been many cases in our day-to-day problem solving in which we have come up with a good solution but failed to plan the action that carries out the solution. For example, we may have created a problem by miscalculating how long it could take to meet a client's order. The client is unhappy, but we still have a chance because we have decided to authorize some overtime. We even call the client and clear the new arrangement, which will make the delivery a little late, but not too late. The client is not too unhappy, but it's a borderline case in which a further delay or foul-up would cause some serious consequences. We present our solution to the people in our organization who we expect to take the responsibility of getting the project underway. We are satisfied that things will work out fine now that we've done a good job of problem solving. Considering the fact that we looked at all the alternatives, picked the one that would keep the client reasonably happy, avoided overloading our own workers, and met our economic and time requirements, it was a good choice. We have reason to be proud. But suppose we forget to do a very good job of planning the action we intended to take. Some time goes by, and we decide to see how things are coming. In disbelief we hear an employee say, "Oh, did you mean for *me* to call the people? I thought that since this was an exception, you'd want to do it yourself." Now it's too late to salvage the project, and there's no way to satisfy the client. Nothing we say is going to sound like we know what we're doing, and that may be a good evaluation of the situation. We failed to consider that, because things were already out of step, we could expect additional mistakes along the way. On any single project, we can usually overcome one problem, even a serious one, but it's difficult to recover if the mistakes we make keep causing other problems. This tells us something about how to deal with the plans we make through the problem-solving process. We should expect things to go wrong and keep working to keep this from happening.

When we come to the final decision about the solution to the problem, we then begin to plan the action. The process is easy to describe, but difficult to watch closely. We need to know *who* is going to be doing *what.* This means that we don't leave anything to chance. We make specific assignments to specific people and make sure they know they have these responsibilities. Not only do we tell them what they're supposed to do, but we also spell out the step-by-step procedures in the action. It may be that time is a part of the action; if it is, we make certain that the time increments for each detail are spelled out. We set the deadlines for everything that has to be done rather than just saying, "Get it done as quickly as possible!" That's too indefinite, and *this isn't the time to be indefinite.* To simplify it, we just spell out this step in the problem-solving process by saying make sure that we let everybody concerned know *who* is going to do something, *what* they're going to be doing, and *when.* If any special considerations or things are to be handled in an unordinary way, we spell that out too, calling attention to it *as an exception.*

Act on the Plan

The best solution to any problem we have will fall apart if we don't actually carry it out. No matter how much we plan and tell people what they're supposed to do and when they're supposed to do it, we may still fail if we don't make a diligent effort to see that things really happen as we've planned them. If there is ever a time when we need the *controlling* function of management, it is at this point. This doesn't mean that we become tyrants, walk behind everybody engaged in any activity connected with the solution, get reports by the hour, or look over people's shoulders and critique every action. It does mean that we build in reporting procedures that tell us when things are finished and when deadlines are met while we do our best to encourage and reinforce those who are working hard to make this project come off all right. It isn't a time to take responsibility away from people; it's a time to let people know we trust them to do their best to reach the prescribed goal. This is the time for *positive thinking.* It's a time to tell our people that they can do it, and do it well.

The word is *trust.* Letting our people know the serious-ness of the situation and that we trust their skill and desire to get the job done is the best thing we can do to build their morale and get them committed. Nothing else will be as effective in motivating them to accomplish the difficult tasks we have assigned them.

We also should be around to offer our support to their effort. As we've already discussed, because it is an un-usual or abnormal activity, we can expect some obstacles to arise. If so, our job is to clear these obstacles out of the way. We have to be able to say to people in other groups that it's all right that our people are doing it this way. Like-wise, higher management must be aware that they may see some slightly unorthodox things happening, but that we have everything under control. We need to figure these things out ahead of time so we'll know what to expect from others and be able to act in time to avoid additional obsta-cles. This not only runs interference for our people so they can do their job, but it also keeps us out of their way while they get on with the work.

CONCLUSION

The supervisor's job is to solve problems. If there weren't some problems, there would be much less use for supervisors. It is better to get our jobs done by *solving the problems* than by waiting for problems to go away. In a perfect environment there would perhaps be no problems, but problems exist because we don't have—and never will have—a perfect place to work, a place where everyone will do the job exactly as it should be done and when and how it should be done. Problems happen because somebody somewhere hasn't done the job correctly. There are some steps that make problem solving more reliable and more satisfying, but if we have to remember all these steps each time we solve even the smallest problem, we'll never get any problems solved. Ideally, we can get the swing of the techniques by practicing on small problems, or even by going back to apply the steps to a problem we've recently solved. In this way we can get a feel for how well we're doing *without* consciously using the steps. This will point up any weaknesses we have and make us more anxious to apply the steps we've discussed in this chapter. There's nothing complicated about the steps and we can learn them easily, but we have to be willing to take the time to use them when we are solving the problems. Being unwilling to give up the time is the main thing that will keep us from using a step-by-step problem-solving technique. We see a problem, get in a hurry, and dive right in, using the first solution that comes to mind. Only after we've handled the situation do we take time to analyze our actions and even say to ourselves, "I wonder why I did it that way?" or, "I wonder why I didn't do it that other way?"

The simple steps we've covered make sense. Here they are again:

1. Be certain a problem exists
2. Be certain to solve the real problem
3. Gather enough facts to deal with the problem
4. Hold off solving problems as long as possible
5. Find alternate solutions
6. Test possible solutions
7. Plan the action
8. Act on the plan

A final note: When we've solved a problem, small or large, and are satisfied with the results, we should *leave it* and move on to the next problem. We need to avoid making a career out of one problem. It *was* a problem, but it isn't anymore, so it doesn't deserve any more of our time and effort. If it still does need time and energy, then *we still have a problem.* We should forget small problems except for any lessons we can learn from them, but we should think about large problems at least once more to make sure things have completely died down. Rather than thinking of it as returning to the scene of the crime, we should think of it as revisiting the scene of our victory.

DISCUSSION QUESTIONS

1. How is it that in predicting problems with the newer work force we have made them self-fulfilling prophecies?

2. Think about the different ways we react to problems. What should be our first approach?

3. List the steps that should be followed in problem solving.

4. Select a problem you've recently solved and apply these steps. How well did you do without consciously following the steps?

5. Now select a potential problem you will have to solve and apply the steps. How does this compare with the information in question 4?

Chapter six

Introducing Change

There are a lot of clichés about change, all of which try to state a simple explanation of how people react to change. We hear things like, "Change is constant," or "The only thing that never changes is that we are always changing," or "People always resist change." As we'll see in this chapter, in some ways all these things are true; however, in other ways they are all quite wrong. There is no doubt that things change constantly, but to many in the organization—especially those new to the work force—things seem to continue in the same way without any improvement. Even though change is constant, it is sometimes subtle and sometimes very drastic, with complete reorganizations rapidly taking place. Perhaps the most misunderstood thing about change is that we blatantly say people resist it, yet complaints that the organization doesn't make one change or another are main topics of conversation at almost every break time. Rarely do we hear employees complaining about change and wanting the organization to keep things just like they are. It is much too simple to say that people will always resist change. The effects of making changes are often deep, lasting, and certainly complex. How do we make changes, though, so that these effects will be positive and not negative? There are some things we can do to make changes work for us. As organizations grow and improve, changing personnel and goals, we must make certain changes in the way we do things. If we understand why change is a problem, we can do a better job of handling the change. In this chapter we'll see what we can learn about the effect of change on people and some steps we can follow to be successful at introducing change.

UNDERSTANDING CHANGE

When we decide to make a change—whether it's moving somebody to another desk, changing to a new procedure, or completely restructuring the organization—we can expect some problems to arise. Is there a problem because people resist change, or is there something different we need to consider? Let's dispel the idea that people resist change just as a matter of course, because change is often a very happy occasion when people are unhappy, frustrated, or confused in the job they're in. How often we hear people react to a change with, "It's about time!" We can also see that people often try to be the first to be in on a change, and most merchandising efforts appeal to this instinct when they say, "Be the first to try this *new* and *different* version of the old product." New cars, new dress styles, and new home designs are some of the many evidences that certain kinds of changes appeal to people. It just is not right, then, to say that people resist change *automatically*.

To get a better idea of predicting the outcome of change, we can classify changes and people to some de-

"I wonder if headquarters has lost our address? There hasn't been a change come through in the policy manual in over two weeks!"

gree. When we say that change that opens up new possibilities is welcomed by those who think they are being stifled in their present situation, we classify both the nature of change and the nature of people. Some change is obviously for the betterment of the people involved, whereas other change is seen as threatening. Some people are satisfied where they are, doing what they're doing, but others are tired or frustrated with their present work and will welcome change. Some changes promise advantages but don't have obvious rewards. Other changes don't seem to offer much advantage, but an in-depth study shows that their implementation results in many good things. There are also changes that provide both the good and the bad, in which some of the results are worthwhile and satisfying even though we pay the price of some undesirable side effects. For example, you are offered a new job doing something that you like to do with an increase in pay; however, you will have to work under a manager that you don't particularly favor and with some people you feel uncomfortable around. In such a situation you are likely to say you have "mixed emotions" about the change.

We can also classify people in several ways. There are those who have weathered changes before and have not found them too threatening; therefore they don't mind them. Others have had some bad experiences with changes, even those that promised good rewards, so they find a degree of threat in any offer of change. For these people, the rewards will have to be very high and the disadvantages very low before they can accept the change readily. There are those who have had difficulty adjusting to various jobs but ultimately find themselves in a situation where everything is going just right. People who have security problems will get very comfortable in their present jobs and will resist even changes that offer much promise of good things and virtually no bad consequences. There are those who get bored being in one environment or job or relationship too long and simply drift from one situation to another, not looking for permanence or security and welcoming change just to get out of a boring situation. Change is just a vehicle to get them to another situation, and they neither like nor dislike the change.

It has not been the objective here to point out all the different kinds of changes or all the different characteristics that cause people to react differently to change. Rather, the point is that change is complex and that when we generalize about it we have to be careful not to oversimplify what we say. We can also see that, because it is difficult to predict how change will be received, it can be considered a problem for an organization. Few among the supervisor's responsibilities can cause as much anxiety among the workers as the changes he or she must implement.

RESENTMENT OF CHANGE

While as a rule people do not resist change, it is accurate to say that most of us resist *being* changed. Very early in life we start resisting when other people tell us what to do. We like to choose our own changes. Left alone, we might make the same change someone else tries to impose on us, but we would rather make the decision to do a certain thing differently than by having someone else tell us to do it. If we are given an opportunity to make the decision ourselves, we do a pretty fair job of accepting the change. If others tell us what our changes are going to be, we may not only resist them, but also try to make the changes fail. If nothing else, our commitment level is certainly very low.

Younger employees will especially resist being changed, particularly if the change seems to be arbitrary or without good reason. They have had a chance to live with change and are usually more ready to accept something different than are those who have been around for a generation longer, but they will resist being forced into doing something different just because someone tells them to do it, without a good reason. On the other hand, this group will respond very quickly to making changes they have a hand in deciding, especially if we let them help us make decisions about their changes. In this situation they will have a very high commitment level. Since they aren't afraid of doing things differently, the change part of the action will either be insignificant as a threat or exciting as a possibility. In either case, their attitude will work in favor of making the change. The problem with this group often develops when the supervisor decides that these employees aren't really interested in much of anything and makes the choices for them. Their unfavorable reaction is interpreted by the supervisor as a "bad attitude" and reinforces the decision not to bring them into the discussion of the changes in their lives and work. Supervisors who have let these employees in on decisions about such changes have discovered that the results are quite satisfactory. This doesn't mean that they will forever be grateful to us because we let them make a decision or two; they will simply accept it as something we should have done anyway and expect us to do it again next time. As supervisors of these working people, we have to be careful not to continue to see ourselves as leaning over backward in our treatment of them, expecting to keep on getting patted on the back for it.

We've used the words "resist being changed" to describe the feeling and reaction of people being forced to change without being a part of the decision. It would also be correct to say that they will *resent* being changed. In other words, not only will they have no commitment to see that the newer ideas or procedures or policies are successful, but they will also actually resent the fact that we've tried to put the new ideas into practice. This resentment causes them to fight against the change and also causes the problems that arise. We may have a perfectly good idea for accomplishing a certain task that requires a change in the present procedures. The reasons for the change are so obvious that we don't bother to discuss it with the employees until it is time to make it. As we tell the employees how things are going to be from now on, we begin to get the feeling that they aren't accepting things as well as we thought they would. They mumble and ask questions that don't seem pertinent. They start to give excuses why the ideas won't work, and we can't understand why they are getting so upset over such a small thing. They seem to be taking it out on us and may even appear to be banding together to resist the changes we're proposing. It is at this point that many people say, "People resist change," because they can see no other reason for such resentment. Had we thought about it, we'd have realized that the resentment wasn't coming from the change itself but from our approach to instituting the change. We may like to blame the employees, but the truth is that we did a poor job of introducing the change.

A LOSS OF SECURITY

Change is often seen by many people as a voyage into the unknown. Those who are secure in their present jobs know where everything is, know whom to call for any kind of action, know when and how to act, and are the most distressed over having to make a change. While to some change represents a challenge, to others it is a threat to their security, and they will oppose any such threat. If we can't read the reactions well enough, we may think that they are resisting the ideas we are proposing; thus we spend an inordinate amount of time trying to justify the idea. They may even offer some opposition in the way of questions and logic that we will try to overcome, not knowing that we are fighting the wrong battle. It isn't the idea that they are objecting to; they would react the same way to any idea that appears to challenge their security. They may not even know that this is their problem; if we suspect this and try to overcome the objections by saying (in essence), "You're just afraid of losing your security," we're in real trouble.

The answer lies in making the idea less threatening to their security, assuring them that much of what they are now doing will still be done in the new procedures and that they will be expected to use their present knowledge, skill and experience to carry out the new procedures. This will help alleviate their fears about the threat of change and allow them to hold on to as much security as possible until they establish a new way to get the security. We can be in real trouble with such people if we start off by telling them that this new assignment is a "real challenge" and that they will have to learn a lot before they will be able to do the job properly. Such an approach will knock the props right out from under them before they even consider the change. In short, if change is involved, we should be careful to whom we offer challenge.

INTRODUCING CHANGE

The principles we will talk about here are just as applicable to small changes as they are to large ones, but we can get away with doing things a little less according to the rules when we're dealing with small changes with one or two employees. When we're talking about major changes that involve many employees, we can't take a chance of doing it in a sloppy way. The following steps should be considered in planning for change. Just as in problem solving, we can't take the time to go through a rigid set of rules every time we suggest to somebody that they use a different typewriter or sit in a different kind of chair. In the case of major changes, though, we can and should take the time to do careful planning. This will do more to head off problems than anything else. Let's talk about the steps in this planning.

1.   Justify the changes to ourselves.   If we can't justify the changes we're getting ready to make to our own thinking, we probably shouldn't make the changes. The decision to make is whether the changes will benefit the total organization, including the employees we supervise. If not, we may still need to make the changes, but it will be more difficult to do it without too much trouble. It is never justifiable to make a change simply to shake people up or to vary things that have been static too long. It may sound good when we say it, but we have enough trouble and problems without looking for more!

2.   Encourage   group   decisions.   We've   already talked about letting the employees in on the decisions about the changes we are considering. We should use their knowledge and experience whenever possible, listen to their suggestions, and be sure they know that their ideas do count, even if we can't use all their suggestions. The more they become involved in planning for the change, the smoother it will go and the better they will receive it when it comes; also, there's a good chance that they will begin to look for other changes that offer improvements to the operation. When this happens, we have the best of all worlds—employees looking for change, and no problem with introducing it.

3.   Keep employees informed.   When we bring the employees in on the problem of possibly making a change, we need to give them as much information as possible about the reasons for the change. In addition, as the change becomes imminent, we should give them everything they need to know to understand why it is being made. In fact, the first thing to do is tell them *why* the change is taking place. If we've done the job correctly, we won't have to spend much time with this because the employees will have been involved in it from the beginning and will know why the change is necessary. We should also tell them just *who* will be affected by this change. The people who are going to be involved, even indirectly, should be told exactly how they will be affected and to what extent. As we'll see later, telling the employees *when* the change is to take place will stop much of the speculation. The time of the change shouldn't be too far away from the time the information about it is given.

4. Use a positive approach.   Part of the positive approach is to show that the results will be such an improvement that the time of the introduction will be immediate. However, it is most important to show the benefits that can be derived from the changes. We should be sure that most of the benefits aren't for the organization and only a few for the employees. However, we shouldn't hide the benefits for the organization, because the employees are smart enough to know that we don't just sit aound and think of ways to make things better for them without regard for the organization's welfare. We sometimes make the mistake of beginning to introduce the change with an apology for whatever problems it is going to cause. This makes it very hard to show the benefits to the employees after we've as much as told them that this isn't going to make them very happy.

5. Avoid the rumor mill.   We've already seen that the introduction should include the important information and that the change should begin as soon as possible after we tell the employees about it. One benefit of this approach is to avoid rumors. If we fail to give the employees the pertinent data, they will fill in the rest with rumors, wrong con-

clusions, and speculations. If we wait too long to begin
instituting the change, that time will be filled in with additional rumors about the reasons for the delay, and everything will soon be out of proportion.

6. Inform key people early. Key people in most organizations can help a great deal if they know what we
plan to do and why. It is frequently to our advantage to
keep these employees informed along the way, even if we
have to ask them to keep the information in confidence for
a while. We need their help and support when the introduction is made; therefore it is important that they *know this*
ahead of time so that their commitment level will be high at
the time of the introduction.

7. Deal with questions openly. When we finally announce the change, we should provide ample time for
questions. There are, however, some key things we need to
remember as they are being asked, or the questions and
answers will lead us into more trouble instead of getting us
off the hook. Of course, the worst thing we can do is to
avoid a question altogether. If we leave ourselves open for
a question, we need to deal with it or give a legitimate reason for not answering it. If we don't know the answer, we
should offer to find it and then *be sure to follow through.*
The next mistake that will cause trouble is to become defensive about an answer. If we start to get upset over a
question, the group will know it and begin to wonder why
we can't just answer the question without getting bothered
about it. We should give whole, honest answers to the
questions or not answer them at all. There are legitimate
reasons why we can't reveal some information, and we can
even say that we're sorry but that's something we'll have to
tell them later. We should leave it there, promise to give
them an answer as soon as we can, and then go to the next
question. If we do decide to give them an answer, though,
we should make it as much of the answer as we can (with-

out prolonging the discussion) and make sure that we haven't left them with a false idea just to avoid further questions. Sooner or later they'll find the truth and will know that we didn't give them the whole truth. Then they will justifiably start to lose confidence in us and will not respond very favorably to the new ideas or changes we are proposing.

8. Don't play games. Part of the effort to be totally honest with employees is to avoid playing games with them about the changes. If we know something and can tell them, then we should; if we can't, we shouldn't go around like a small child who says to a friend, "I know something you don't know, and I'm not going to tell you!" This is especially true if the results of the change are going to be unfavorable to the employees. We shouldn't make it sound like all kinds of good things are about to transpire for them if it isn't going to be that way. Rather, we should simply tell them the truth: "This job is being eliminated because of a cutback in budget . . . ," or "We are going to shift the responsibility for this to the other group because they have more people who are trained to handle it."

Once we've made the announcement and dealt with the questions, we should terminate the discussion and get on with the action. Some employees will deal with a new idea until they make a problem out of it, but we can avoid this by getting on with other business and starting the action on this change as soon as possible. If all we've said is, "Sometime in the next several months we plan to institute certain changes," we deserve any problems we get as a result!

CONCLUSION

Change is often necessary to get the job done correctly, and in making changes we should use the steps discussed in this chapter. We try to avoid change just for the sake of change. We should think of change as a positive part of our job; we can make it that if we handle the change correctly. Perhaps the single most important thing we can do in introducing change is to realize that some kind of conflict is quite possible, even though we don't see how or why. Getting the employees involved in the discussion ahead of time, keeping them informed, and dealing with their questions honestly will help smooth over the introduction. Using the employees' input in the beginning may even make some of the change unnecessary, and we will at least have their commitment when the change does come. Generally, the newer employees are more conditioned to change than the older ones, but they are also more critical when it comes to looking for reasons for the change, for the most part because they aren't steeped in the tradition of the older employees who say, "But we've always done it *this* way." If we're successful in introducing change often enough, we'll hear our employees saying, "There must be a better way, since we've always done it this way!"

DISCUSSION QUESTIONS

1. Discuss the validity of the clichés about change, such as: "change is constant," "the only thing that never changes is that we are always changing," or "people always resist change."
2. What are some reasons for negative responses to change?
3. How can we make changes with positive results?
4. List some steps to be considered when introducing a change.

Chapter seven

Handling Poor Performers

All workers do satisfactory work some of the time; in fact, even the worst ones probably do much that is right most of the time. The fact that they are still employed suggests that their supervisors have been more than just tolerant with unsatisfactory employees. However, no employee ever does work that is completely satisfactory *all the time*. Therefore, if this chapter is to make any sense, we need a definition of the poor performer or the "unsatisfactory" employee. The unsatisfactory worker is one who meets one of these conditions.

1. The work is sometimes not up to a measurable expressed standard.
2. The work is consistently not up to this standard.
3. Normal efforts at correcting this below-standard performance do not suffice.

We'll extend this definition further as we get into the discussion, but for now let's deal only with the last item. "Normal efforts" are actions taken with any or all of the other employees who fall below a stated standard, under similar conditions.

From the definition we can see that we aren't talking about that occasional foul-up or miscue or about the employee who infrequently hits a snag in which everything seems to go wrong. Usually in these cases the employees themselves will either do a pretty good job of shaking off the problems, or go to their supervisors for help in training or counseling. We will be discussing the following:

1. How do we determine unsatisfactory performance?

2. What are some of the possible causes of this poor performance?

3. What are the processes available for dealing with these employees?

4. What are the differences in the ways the younger employees and the older employees react to correction procedures?

5. How can we turn the action into a positive supervisory force?

SETTING THE STANDARD

What is a "standard" of performance? We will talk a lot about standards in this chapter, so we should define the term. First, let's see what a standard *is not*. It isn't the performance you get or have got from the best performing employee who ever worked for you in this particular assignment. A look at these employees will show that their performance was above what you think you can get from your average employees. Also, these employees were most often raised to a higher level of work, since they were performing *above* what was expected of them on this job. There are several obvious reasons why their performance can't be the standard, including the facts that you will never get very many people to meet that standard and that you won't be able to reward all this exceptional behavior.

Just as we can't choose our best performer as the standard, neither can we choose an average employee's performance and decide that we'll just let that be the standard. It sounds attractive to do it this way because it seems very fair. After all, the standard should be in the reach of most of the employees, and it isn't asking too much of the people to be just average. What, then, is the problem? Every time we hire a new employee, *the average changes.* If we have a large number of poor performers, the average expectation is low; if we have a large number of excellent performers, the average is high. Actually, we don't usually set standards like this, but it ends up being the same thing. We appraise our people as being good or bad by looking at the other employees around them to see how they all match up. In the absence of a standard, the end result is a standard that fluctuates, depending on what other employees do.

We certainly cannot set the standard according to the performance of the least productive employee, reasoning that since we keep this employee, all the other employees would have to be meeting the standard. Therefore, if we don't set the standard by the best employee, the average of all the employees, or the lowest performer, how do we set it? A standard is what has been decided on, without looking at the people on the job, as a reasonable expectation from the employees with regard to time, production, job abilities and training, and the amount of money we're willing to pay for the job.

WHO SETS THE STANDARD?

There are many ways of setting standards, some better than others. Supervisors often inherit standards from their predecessors. They have no say in setting the standards, but they are expected to see that the employees meet them. If there is no change in personnel other than the new supervisor, and if the work has been progressing well under the existing set of standards, then there's nothing wrong with them.

Standards are also set by experienced supervisors who, separately or with design or industrial engineers, use an autocratic approach and arbitrarily set a group of standards for a specific job. ("Arbitrarily" here means without consulting the employees doing the job.) This sounds like a poor way of setting standards, but actually under certain circumstances it is very sensible. When a large number of employees do fragmented pieces of the total job without total knowledge of what has to be done, supervisors need to set the standards. At least, those who have access to the total job and know how it is to be done should decide how the job should be measured—hence, set the standards.

A third way standards are set is by a joint effort of supervisors and members of the work force. Undoubtedly, this method will get the most commitment from the employees, but it also involves some very obvious drawbacks. If the supervisors already know how a job should be done (how well and how quickly), they already know what the standards are; thus they risk being in a selling position, in which they try to convince the employees to buy into the standards they have already set. Since the supervisors don't want the employees to know that there are standards, they end up playing games rather than contributing to a mature joint effort to come up with proper standards. Also, there is the chance that the employees never will come up with the same standards and the supervisors have to be ready either to give on some points or to turn arbitrary. The newer workers will spot this game playing more quickly than others will, and they will see in it a kind of hypocrisy that they have learned to distrust and resent.

The joint effort has some advantages, though, and we shouldn't overlook them. No other approach to supervising yields more cooperation and commitment from the workers than including them in the decision-making process. They feel like they are an important part of the operation and that they are significant in helping set goals and objectives. Everything we know about setting standards tells us that this method will come nearest not only to getting the standards set high but also to *getting the standards met.* As employees are involved in setting the standards for their own job, they somehow feel that they can do more. In fact, we actually have to be careful that they don't set standards so high that future employees, who weren't involved in the exercise, will wonder how they got so high and even rebel against them. Once we start on this route, we need to stick with it, continuing to let the employees in on what we plan to do and how we plan to reach the goals. We must constantly remind the employees that the standards are theirs, and make it sort of a contest to see if they think the standards are still valid.

The newer working people will respond especially well to this approach—if we handle it maturely and do not play games with them. We may not like their frankness about the job or always be ready to accept what they say about some parts of the job that they don't think need to be done. However, once they find that we are serious about wanting their opinion, we can be sure that they will give it to us, set reasonable standards—even high ones—and then do whatever it takes to reach them. We'll have a problem if we think that they aren't serious (and hence won't try to reach

"It occurred to me that maybe I should mention safety to you. Perhaps there is some small misunderstanding?"

the standards) and get in their way by asking them how they're doing, when they'll be finished, and if they still think they can reach the standards. A little bit of this "mistrust" goes a long way with them; when we start it, they'll just cut out and leave it all with us.

We have mentioned that not only will the standards be higher if employees set them, but also that the commitment to meet them will be higher. Having set the standards themselves, the employees will feel both pride in and a challenge to meet them. We can take advantage of this by letting them in on the standards-setting process from the beginning. Of course, much of what has been said so far assumes that standards for the jobs don't already exist. Frequently, they have been in existence for a long time, but even then there are necessary changes in procedures, revisions in policies, or modifications in the equipment. These are the times to get the employees to *help us,* since it is often possible that they will know more about the day-to-day job than we do. We may know what needs to be done and may be able to cite statistics on what has been done in the past, but the employees on the job, who do it every day under working conditions only they can understand, will have more first-hand information than we will ever have. So we do need their help, and we can get it and make good use of it if we do a good job of supervising.

WHO SHOULD BE AWARE OF THE STANDARDS?

It is obvious that the supervisors who must measure the standards and appraise the people doing the work to meet those standards should have a good idea of what the standards are. They should be familiar enough with them to tell if the employees are meeting them. However, if that's all they can do, they still won't be able to do their job as well as they should. Supervisors have the responsibility to train the workers so they can meet the standards. Consequently, if they don't have sufficient *working* knowledge of the standards, they won't be able to. It is the supervisor's job to know the standards well enough to train, appraise, and measure potential for higher levels of performance. Although this requires a fairly deep understanding of the operation we expect of our employees, it does not mean that we should actually be able to outperform every worker or even be able to do the job up to the standard. (We don't have to be able to outwrestle every worker to prove that we're the boss!) Our job isn't to do the work but to see that others can; and if we find that we don't know how to do the work well enough to train others, then we must find somebody who does (even if it's another one of our employees) and see that the training gets done. Of course, we still need to know enough to see that the training is done properly and meets the standard.

The workers need to know the standards, too; if they don't, we can hardly be fair in our appraisals. If they don't know the standards we're using to measure them, there's little chance they will be able to meet them—*at least on purpose.* We've already seen that the employees need to know the standards; obviously, they need to know not only what the standards are, but also *how to reach them.* That is the supervisor's job—to train them or *see that they get trained.*

Finally, those in levels above us need to know something about the standards, and it's our job to see that they have this information. Even though we don't try to hide anything from them, we need to be careful about giving them too much information, because they don't need to be able to work any of the equipment, handle the job, or even supervise others who do it. That's our job. They *do* need to know something about what we expect from our people and how we set these standards. We can give this information to them in capsule form and then answer any question that comes up about the job. This will also help them in their long-range planning efforts, and perhaps it will help us when we need more people, more time, more materials, and so on.

So far we've spent a lot of time talking about standards; we've seen who sets them, why we have them, and who should know them. But what does all this have to do with supervising the poor performer? Before we leave the matter of standards, we should point out that many studies show that a majority of people who are performing below standard are *unaware of it* and are especially unaware of their supervisors' expectations of them. When it comes to doing their job, they just don't know *how well, how much,* or *how often.* Many experiments have been done in which supervisors were asked what they expected of their people and their people were asked what they thought their supervisors expected of them. The answers have rarely ever matched. In the next part of this chapter we'll discuss why people don't do their jobs as well as they should.

WHY PEOPLE DON'T PERFORM

After we've set all the standards and informed and trained all our people, we'll still find that not all of them will perform up to these standards. As we'll see here, there are many reasons for this.

1. They don't know what to do. We've already seen that one of the main reasons people don't do their jobs as they should is that they just don't know what to do. It may be that we have failed to train them by either not telling them or not demonstrating what is expected of them. If we don't tell them, yet expect them to do the job well, we're doing a poor job of communicating and we're being unfair. We're expecting too much of them if we don't see that they have the job demonstrated in the correct way. Unclear standards may also be a problem; they may be stated or explained in such a way that the employees are confused and uncertain about what they're expected to do. Finally, there is a problem when standards simply don't exist. There is constant confusion with "floating" standards, by which we seem to expect something different each day and the employees stay confused and frustrated all the time.

2.   They don't know how they're doing. Even when good standards have been set, they won't do much good if we fail to let the employees know how well they're doing on the job. Employees work on the job every day, and on each of these days they are either meeting or missing the standards to some extent. Both workers and supervisors would go crazy trying to keep each employee informed every day about how well he or she is doing on each task. There are few jobs for which this would make any sense at all. This doesn't mean that the employees can't know where they stand with regard to the standards or that they should be surprised at appraisal time. There's no need for them to go for very long without being told how well they are performing. We should realize that feedback breaks down in several ways when it comes to keeping employees informed about their progress. First, we just don't bother to find out how well they're doing; then even if we do find out, we don't bother to tell them. A poor appraisal system can also be a problem. There's not enough space here to analyze all the things necessary to get a good appraisal system going, but suffice it to say that whatever system we use should make the standards relate to the everyday job. One example will suffice: We put a heavy emphasis on such things as *attitude* and *willingness to work,* for which we can set no measurable standard; then we forget that the day-to-day activities are filled with measurable tasks. We can't judge employees by intangible attitudes and ignore the production side of the job.

3.   Poor job design. If we have unrealistic standards, we shouldn't expect employees to meet them. We can expect a great deal of unreality to get into the standards if they have been set by a committee of people who meet away from the job and don't know very much about what it's like to be on the front line of production every day. They may even set conflicting standards, which will frustrate both us and the employees. For example, one standard may say that the customer always comes first, and another may say that the employee must handle as many customers as possible. When the employee follows the first standard and devotes time to satisfy a particularly difficult-to-please customer, he or she is automatically violating the second standard.

4.   Improper reward system. It is almost trite to say that people are more likely to repeat things for which they are rewarded or reinforced. If employees do things well and we praise them or give them some kind of recognition, there's a good chance they'll repeat their behavior. If they fail to get rewarded, there's less of a chance that they'll do it as well or as often again. To go a step further, if we react in a way that they perceive as threatening or punishing, there is much less chance that they will repeat their behavior again. If all of this is used properly, things work well for us. If it isn't used well, it can give us poor performance. For example, if we reward the employees for doing things incorrectly, they will continue to do the wrong things. If the standard says that a job should be done by going through certain steps but the employee gets done more quickly by taking short cuts—and gets praised by the supervisor for finishing early—the reward is for the wrong thing. This behavior will probably repeat itself as long as the praise is there, and the employee will be very frustrated when he or she is suddenly evaluated as unsatisfactory for doing the work in the very way the supervisor has been praising. In the same manner, if the employee goes through the proper steps but is criticized by the supervisor for not getting the job done more quickly (instead of getting praised for doing it according to the standard), the employee sees this as punishment for correct behavior. The result is that the good behavior will diminish rather quickly.

5. Mismatch between the employee and the job. There are many examples in the work world in which we manage to get the wrong employee in the job; this results in poor performance. It may not be that the employee cannot do the job, but just that the supervisor hasn't done a very good job of picking someone with the proper temperament or interest. For example, we may fill a job that requires creativity with someone who is very highly organized, systematic, and quite capable of doing well-planned jobs, but who is not very good at handling the less standardized operations. Or we may assign a very highly structured job that has to be done exactly the same way every time to an imaginative person who is quick to see better ways of doing things and can adjust to the "unknown" without losing a sense of security. Either case is a mismatch and in the long run will probably end in poor performance.

6. Lack of motivation. This is often a "catch-all" expression that takes care of all the other reasons why people don't do their jobs. It includes malcontents, lazy employees, and employees who have lost their enthusiasm, are bitter, or have outside interests. Since motivation is such a difficult thing to measure and is influenced by so many things, we'll save the discussion of it until we get to the chapter on motivation. Let's just say here that even though we may never know why employees aren't motivated or even why they don't perform properly, we shouldn't quit trying to find out why and to get them to do their job as they should. If we go through the steps of finding out and trying to deal with it and still fail, we can assure ourselves that we have done the best we could and perhaps even gone beyond what would have been expected of us, considering the performance we are getting. On the other hand, if we're successful, we have to say it was well worth it!

MEASURING POOR PERFORMANCE

After we have established a good set of standards, explained them to the employees, and done the necessary training, we then face the task of measuring to see if the standards are being met. It won't be our purpose here to talk about measuring processes, but we will talk about some important things that we should do in our measuring efforts. First of all, by far the most important aspect of measuring is being certain to measure everyone by the same standard. The reasons are so obvious that we need not talk about them; any inconsistency in this area will destroy any success we expect to have in dealing with unsatisfactory employees. As a result of all they've heard about how organizations are run, the new workers often come into the organization *expecting* to get unfair treatment; thus, they will very quickly pick up on any action on our part that proves that expectation. Being innocent won't excuse us if we somehow reason our way into using different standards for different people. If we expect one employee to sell a certain amount, see a certain number of clients, or service a certain number of accounts within a given time, we need to hold everybody to the same standard. We can't let a good-attitude, bad-salesperson employee get away with less, or excuse an employee with an alcoholic grandmother. We may set up quotas depending on the kind of work or territory to be handled, but the standard is set by the work or territory, not the employee in that job.

Another part of this inconsistency is treating the same employee with different standards at different times. If we set standards for the job, not the employee, then the measuring will be done the same every time we look at an employee doing the job, whoever is in the job and whenever we look at him or her. We will never get a satisfactory standard as long as we fail to be consistent in our dealings with our employees. If one day we allow the employee to make more errors in filling out sales slips than on another day, she or he is soon confused about the allowable number of errors. This often happens when we don't watch the quotas as closely as we should. We don't realize we're behind, and we let the employees go along without much concern with meeting standards until there is a big rush to meet a deadline, and we suddenly expect them to work up to the standard. Also, we don't pay much attention to safety (letting the employees do things in ways that aren't according to the designated safety codes) until there is an accident or an inspection; then we get excited and start citing people for not working according to the safety standards. These inconsistencies mark us as poor supervisors, and we will have a hard time enforcing standards, no matter how well they are spelled out or how well the employees are trained.

One consideration that is sometimes overlooked is that frequently the employee who doesn't meet the standard at one time isn't necessarily working below standard. We have to give sufficient time in our observation to make that decision. Unless the task is very clear and easy and is something the employee has been trained to do and has done for a good while, doing something wrong one or two times isn't poor performance. If the job is something that should be done correctly every time because it is easy and only carelessness will cause it to be done wrong, falling short once or twice in a row is unnecessary and represents a situation where we should get concerned in a hurry. It is different, though, for difficult tasks that aren't done very often. This may mean that the employee has forgotten or needs practice to be able to perform properly. This all means that we should give the employee enough time during the observation for us to see if the problem is a lack of concentration, disinterest, or the need to get familiar with the operation all over again.

While we are observing employees at work, we will do well to let them know we're watching them. Some think this will make them perform better so that we won't catch them doing something wrong, and this is exactly why we should let them know. We aren't trying to sneak up on employees to play "Gotcha!" We shouldn't even be that much of a threat to them, and they ought to know that we are interested in their performance all the time. If we suspect they aren't doing their job as well as they should, we simply say, "I want to take a look at your work more closely to see how it's going. We'll watch it for a couple of days and then I'll let you know what it looks like." It's just that simple and no big deal if neither threats nor promises are made. When we do look at performance, our motivation ought to be to *find something good, not bad.* Hoping they are doing their work satisfactorily, we look for what they're doing well as much as what they're doing poorly, even if we do find something unsatisfactory. Whatever we find, we should *share the information* with the employees as soon as we decide how well they are doing. As we've said before, we don't want to be in the habit of playing games to keep them guessing. If we know something about their performance, they deserve to know it, too!

DEALING WITH POOR PERFORMANCE

For a number of reasons, supervisors often dread dealing with unsatisfactory employees. It would be ideal if all employees were to do their jobs correctly all the time, but we've seen that this isn't going to be the case, so we have to take whatever action is required. Ideally, we will be good enough at diagnosing the problem for our action to provide a satisfactory solution to that problem. It shouldn't be something we dread; however, because it has the aura of "discipline," we don't feel comfortable.

The best approach is to attack the problem head on, rather than putting it off because we dread it. Any problem not dealt with as it occurs runs a better-than-average chance of getting bigger. The key words are not only those we talked about earlier, such as "fair" and "firm" but also "mature" and "unemotional." We should avoid acting like a parent who is disciplining a disobedient child, for it is a mature adult who has failed to meet a specified standard. After we've decided that we can no longer tolerate the below-standard activity and determined that the cause is not a lack of understanding or training, we then should take action, which is, in fact, a form of discipline. If we think the employee will never be able to perform satisfactorily, we have no choice but to remove him or her from the job, either by a move to another job or by dismissal. If the employee will stay on the job but will be subject to discipline, we should take the necessary steps to practice what we'll call "progressive discipline," which is dealing with the employee's poor performance in progressively more severe ways. For example, we start off with an explanation of the standard, letting the employee know what we expect and the consequences of not meeting the standard. If there is another violation, we take the first action we mentioned, perhaps a written reprimand in the employee's personnel record. If this doesn't achieve the desired reaction (or action) we take the next step, which may be suspension for several days. Each time we explain our expectations and the consequences of missing the mark further—not as a threat but simply as a matter of record so there will be no misunderstanding if there is need for further discipline. We should never threaten anything we aren't *prepared* to carry out or that we don't have the *authority* to carry out. We should take the time to document the things that have happened and our comments on what will happen if the performance doesn't improve, and we should let the employee know what we have documented and how we've done it. In this way everything is aboveboard, and we should continue to look for *improvement,* not failure. The goal is to get the job done, not to get rid of an employee. Any employee who is already on the job, even one who has not met the standards, is a better investment than a replacement, *if* the employee will perform up to standard. It costs a lot of time, effort, and money to hire and train a new employee; and it is not much of an investment when we aren't completely certain that the performance we'll get will be any better than what we already have.

PERFORMANCE DEFICIENCY AND THE NEWER EMPLOYEES

Dealing with the newer workers is the area in which we are most apt to find difficulty. When we begin to discipline these people, we may get a number of different reactions, many of which we aren't prepared to deal with maturely. This is the group of people who will require as much rational effort on our part as possible. In their words, "We had better keep our cool," or we'll be in trouble. Even in the face of obviously poor performance that has been documented and discussed, we may find that the employees become very resentful and even sullen when we mention it. They may not be very willing to discuss it, and getting little satisfaction from trying to talk to them about their behavior may make us take more drastic steps than we had planned. Here we are in danger of losing our composure and acting less than mature. It may come to using threats, not because we have justification but because we are trying to get some kind of reaction from them. If they don't respond, we get unhappy; if they do react, but sullenly or resentfully, we get angry. In our frustration we take it out on the employee, then spend much of our time trying to explain to our boss why we took that action.

There are those who will appreciate the action we take and will be glad to know that we care enough about them to give them an opportunity to correct their performance without more drastic action. The problem is that this may be the first time many of these people have had much meaningful discipline. They are learning a new pattern, which they are trying to fit into their value system. Since it is discipline, they won't like it very much and will resent it or act sullen. And since they are for the most part a very open group, they may even let us know just how they feel. We will do well to be just as open with them, letting them know how we feel, but without emotion. It is hard to make a distinction between liking their performance and liking them, or letting them know that just because we don't like their performance doesn't mean that we don't like them as people. We must get across the message that says, "When you act in this manner, it makes me feel good," and "When

you act this way, it makes me feel bad.'' Most of these employees have grown up developing very close relationships with people, and they also have tied liking their actions to liking them. We'll have to teach them a new
reaction to being told, ''Because I like having you here, it
makes me feel bad when you don't perform as you know
you should.'' We must have patience to make this work in
the long run, but it's worth it. It will allow us to get the job
done, and that's a good reward for us anytime. It isn't easy,
and for most it will be a new challenge but well worth it.

Whatever our action, especially with the newer working
people, we must strive to *make it a positive experience;*
this is one of the main reasons for being unemotional and
rational in our action. We want to be able to say that here's
a chance for everybody involved to grow and become better people for it; if we can bring it off properly, we will find
such experiences satisfying. The employees can get this
same satisfaction, too, if we handle them properly. Ideally,
we can act in a normal way without procrastinating, deal
with the problem, and move on to the next one without
making the employee feel that we have any hard feelings
toward him or her as a result of the routine action we took.
The employee should look back and see that things
worked out for the best. We should continue to let the employee handle things of importance, do the job with freedom, and learn that we aren't still thinking about the action
that transpired.

CONCLUSION

Employees don't always perform as we'd like them to.
When they don't achieve designated standards, we sometimes have to take action to get them performing as we'd

like them to. Of course, if we have no standards, we can't really blame the employee who performs poorly. However, if there are standards that are reasonable for the type of employees we are hiring, we have every reason to expect the employees to meet them. It is bad when employees fail to do their jobs as well as they are paid to do them, but it is even worse when they don't do their jobs and we don't do anything about it. Correcting behavior is part of our job as supervisors, and we should take definite steps to change the behavior. Since the new behavior is going to make better employees, everybody stands to gain. One important facet of our job is to make sure that everyone knows that this is so, hence making it a positive and rewarding experience. That's part of the *power of positive supervision.*

DISCUSSION QUESTIONS

1. Define the poor performer or the "unsatisfactory" worker.
2. What is a "standard" of performance? State what it is *not* first.
3. Who sets the standard?
4. What are some of the reasons that people don't perform well?
5. How can we measure a poor performer? What is the most effective way to deal with the problem?
6. Discuss the different reactions we get to discipline.
7. What are some things we can do to make disciplinary action a positive experience?

Chapter eight

Motivating Employees

So far this book has made a lot of promises about what would be said and the solutions that would be given in this chapter, but this isn't going to be a panacea chapter. The book pointed out in the beginning that the answer to the problems of supervision, especially of the newer workers, doesn't lie in one single activity or under one chapter heading. In fact, in some ways this chapter may add to the mystery rather than solve it. In the process of laying out what we know about motivation, we may discover that we don't know more things than what we do not know. All is not lost though, because we'll at least clarify some things and get some direction that we need in order to motivate our employees.

There are some things we have to accept and believe before we can fully understand motivation. They aren't all easy to believe, and we may think the rules have many exceptions. This may be the case, but nevertheless it is important for us to enter a study of motivation with some basic beliefs:

157

1. We must believe that workers can be motivated.
2. We must believe that they can like their jobs, whatever they are.
3. We must believe that workers would rather do their jobs correctly than incorrectly.
4. We must believe that with all employees and all conditions taken into consideration, the exceptions to these things are just that—exceptions.

This may be asking a lot from those who haven't supervised before, and perhaps even more from those who have supervised for many years, but everything we know about people suggests that these statements are valid. As we go through this chapter, the meaning of these things will become clearer, and we will see how we can use this information.

WHAT IS MOTIVATION?

When we start talking about motivation, we begin to think about words like "incentives," "goals," and "enthusiasm." These things are all connected with motivation, but we probably need a simple definition to use in this chapter. For our purposes, we'll just say that motivation is some kind of drive or impulse that causes an employee to do a job. If we talk about a "motivated" employee, we're talking about an employee who has a drive that produces effort toward getting the job done. If we talk about trying to motivate an employee, we're talking about doing something that will influence her or him to be enthusiastic or to have some drive toward producing the work.

We all understand that motivation is both external and internal—or, as we will hear psychologists say, "extrinsic" and "intrinsic." There are those who say that it isn't possi-

"Do you wonder why they complain about working so hard during the day and then leave, moving twice as fast as they came in?"

ble to motivate a person, that it must all come from within. However, the kind of motivation we're talking about doesn't fit this category: If we tell an employee to do a job or else be fired and if that employee does the job, then we can say we've motivated him or her. The motivation, at least the original action that produced the drive, came from without, not from within. Mark Twain is supposed to have said that work is "whatever a body is *obliged* to do—play consists of whatever a body is not obliged to do." Undoubtedly, we have to provide some external motivation for some people to get them to be enthusiastic about their jobs. "When you finish this, you can knock off for the rest of the day" is a form of external motivation. It's an incentive plan that tells the employee that the reward comes after the work is over, not during the work itself. "Here's a challenge for you; see if you can make this thing work" is an effort at internal motivation, with the enthusiasm coming from the work itself. The line is fine, however, and we may not always know whether the motivation came from doing the job, completing the job, or not having to fool with the job anymore. The important thing to realize is that it is possible to provide an opportunity for the employees to become enthusiastic or "motivated." Of course, the internal motivation is perhaps more powerful and longer lasting, but since we never know for sure which of these is operating at any given time, we shouldn't trust only in this form of motivation.

ARE PEOPLE DIFFERENT?

We don't have to be around many supervisors very long before we hear one or more say, "The trouble is that everybody's different." Is that true? If so, then, is there any hope in setting basic rules for motivation? Let's examine the statement more closely, noting the comparisons:

1. Not everything is interesting to everybody. To one person, a job that is routine and recurring is pure *drudgery.* To another person such a job represents the best form of *security,* and he or she wouldn't want anything changed.

2. Not everybody likes difficult and challenging jobs. To one person a difficult job is an exciting *challenge;* to another such a job is full of threats and frustrations.

3. Not everybody likes to do the same thing all the time. To one person a repetitive job offers a chance to sharpen skills and master a job; to another such tasks reek of monotony and boredom.

4. Not everybody enjoys working with people. To one person interacting frequently with others on the job is interesting and fun; another may find human relationships painful and confusing.

5. Not everyone likes to stand in front of people and talk or run meetings. To one person it's a chance to meet ego needs and show what he or she knows about a subject; to another it is frightening and a poor way to judge what he or she knows and understands about a subject.

The list could go on, but the point has been made. We've seen that it takes different things to turn different people on. Motivation isn't something that we can read and produce out of a cookbook on motivation.

HOW DO WE MOTIVATE?

If everybody is turned on by different things, how can we ever hope to motivate any of our employees? Is the situation hopeless? No, because, as we've seen in earlier chapters, it isn't true that everybody is totally different from everybody else. Fortunately for supervisors, people have many characteristics in common, and we know some things about people well enough to make accurate predictions about them and their actions under certain situations. If we can predict behavior, we know that there are some things people have in common. It is to these things that we must give our attention, then, if we hope to use them to motivate our employees.

As we saw earlier in this book, we know certain things for sure about people, and these are the things to use in motivational efforts. Let's review them and see how to use them in supervision.

1. People like to be recognized as being good or better than somebody else at something, and they will often go to great lengths to prove that they are better.

2. Everybody likes to be recognized for doing a good job. Although some may tend to shy away from the public aspect of the glory, they nevertheless are disappointed when they don't get any recognition for something they have done.

3. People not only enjoy and expect recognition but also resent it when somebody else gets credit for something they have done.

4. People like to think that they are the masters of their own fates when it comes to growing and developing and getting better jobs. They may not want to do anything about growing, but they resent it if they think the organization is keeping them down with a job that is simpler than they can handle.

5. People enjoy the end results of achieving, that is,

being able to step back and observe something they have accomplished on their own.

6. People appreciate getting responsibility when they think it is a compliment to them rather than just more work for which they will be recognized only if things go badly.

7. Things like policy, working conditions, benefits, and even money aren't very long lasting as far as motivation is concerned. Only things that specifically affect employees on the job everyday are important. The presence of *bad* situations is a hindrance, whereas their absence is not a motivator.

8. Recognition, status, and achievement are ways to provide a quick, strong impact on people, but they don't provide much lasting benefit as far as motivation is concerned.

9. Responsibility and the nature of the job itself aren't potent as far as impact is concerned, but they will last much longer as motivation.

10. People tend to become what we expect of them. If we expect them to fail, they are more apt to fail; if we expect them to succeed, they are more likely to do so.

This is a long list, and we needn't go over each item in detail. Much has been writtten about motivation, and most of the writing discusses each of the preceding items in detail. All we need to do is apply them to the everyday job to make the best use of the information. This list is our toolbox for building the kind of organization we want, regardless of what kind of organization we have or who the employees are.

WHAT DON'T WE KNOW ABOUT MOTIVATION?

It would seem natural that we would know more about what we don't know than about what we do know, but such isn't the case. The preceding list is pretty good and fairly thorough, and it certainly gives us plenty to shoot for as far as motivating people. If we were able to use all the things all the time, we wouldn't have many problems with motivation; but of course we don't use them all, and therein lies the problem. It is one of the things we don't know about. We don't know when to use all this information because, as of yet, we don't have enough tools to tell us which information to use at given times. We can't read people well enough to know whether they are ready for responsibility or if they still need constant recognition. We know that people's needs change, but we aren't always sure if they've changed in their need for stature to the point where they are ready to accept a challenging assignment that could lead to some very good achievement rewards.

To compound what we don't know, we find that people themselves rarely know just what their needs are. For example, few people will admit that they have a driving need for recognition, but most people—at one time or another—have a very strong need for it. The problem here is one of introspection, and in Chapter 12 we'll talk about some of the difficulties connected with this. People just don't know when they're ready for responsibility or if they are in need of growing and achieving, and they may even misinterpret their feelings. They may seek responsibility as a way of getting the recognition they need. The small child who follows his dad around the yard wanting to push the lawnmower isn't interested in taking on the responsibility of grass cutting; he just wants the recognition of being big enough to do what Daddy is doing.

Another confounding aspect is the fact that we aren't always certain just what recognition is; and to make matters worse, it may change from time to time. What is a status symbol at one time may not be later. Wearing a name badge can be a status symbol, if no one else has the right to wear one; when everyone has one, it naturally becomes a drudgery to wear it. However, other things affect the status of the badge. Wearing one may indicate status because only a few people have one; but if a customer thinks the badge is a symbol of a trainee, there goes the status. The trouble is that we can't always predict what will be seen as a form of status or recognition. We may decide that giving somebody a certain job or work location is a form of recognition, but it isn't a status symbol if the other workers don't see it as one. The trouble is that we can't *make* something status just by calling it such. To be true recognition, it must be desired by a number of employees but given to only a few. As soon as everybody has it, it loses its status and is no longer a form of recognition, unless some in other departments want it and don't have it.

This uncertainty keeps us from using the things mentioned earlier in our efforts to motivate our people to a greater degree. If we allow ourselves, we will fall into the trap of saying, "See, this motivation won't work after all, so why bother?" But that's not true. It will and does work, and we are poor supervisors if we don't take advantage of the things we know for sure about people and what motivates them. The point here is that, unfortunately, there are still some things we can't tell about people; this handicaps us but does not completely stifle us. As we get more experience in supervision and dealing with people, we can learn to handle these things more effectively.

MOTIVATION AND THE NEW WORKER

In an earlier chapter we said that fortunately the new workers are no different from the older ones in so far as what motivates them. This means that the list of things we know about people is a good, practical one to which we can go for help with the newer as well as the older workers. This is good news, but we must remember that with the newer workers our problem is compounded by a combination of what we don't know about motivation (as just discussed) and what we don't know about the newer workers. Together, these two unknowns make it harder to decide when to use what method and prevent us from being totally accurate in our predictions. If we'd let ourselves, we could overcome the problem of feeling that these new workers are so totally different that nothing we know applies to them. They aren't all *that* different. They respond the same way to most of the things we've talked about; and if all we do is treat them exactly like we do every other worker we've ever had, we'll have pretty much the same reaction. However, they are different in some ways, as we've discussed at length in the earlier chapters, especially in their values and attitudes toward traditional things. This makes it difficult when it comes to figuring out what they consider to be recognition. At first we may have a hard time deciding whether they consider something valuable, since in many cases their value system is quite different. Being asked to work overtime was once a sign of prestige, but a new worker may consider it punishment. Being told that a suspension is in the offing was once a threat, but a newer worker may think it sounds like a good chance to get some time off with no feeling of threat or embarrassment.

Of all the times when supervisors need to be alert to human reactions, this is the most important. We need to see what happens when we offer a chance for what we consider responsibility, recognition, or achievement. We haven't done our job completely when we just say, "I tried it and it didn't work." We must analyze and find out why it didn't work. We may even get into a frank discussion with the workers to see how they felt about the action we took. For example, we may say that we had hoped that our action would be perceived as positive reinforcement and that we wonder what went wrong. We may not like what we hear in the way of a frank response, but we will do well to listen. *Because of their frankness,* this group can teach us more than any other we have working for us, so we should take advantage of the opportunity when it comes. The beauty of the situation is that we can make the opportunity for open discussion, whereas we've usually had to wait for other employees to decide to tell us how they feel. However, if we don't listen and don't use the information, we'll cut the flow of information quicker with the new work force than with the other employees.

As we've discussed earlier, a job isn't everything to these new workers, and that's a feeling that makes them differ from older employees. In the past we've been able to motivate employees somewhat by letting them have more and more responsibility. Responsibility will motivate the younger working people, but they aren't likely to separate their personal lives from the job. Their priorities are often such that they will think about the job in terms of their personal lives, their families, their hobbies, and their outside activities, rather than the other way around. We have to be careful, then, when we start to use things about the job to make them enthusiastic about their work. When they're on the job, the job itself is still the best place to find motivators, and recognition, responsibility, status, achievement, and challenge are the places where we can get the most motivation. However, if these are perceived as interfering with personal plans, the motivation factors may be low, especially early in the work experience. As the employee gets more and more satisfaction from the job, receives more experiences that are satisfying, and sees that it feels good to work well, then her or his personal life will have less and less draw.

The single most critical element in dealing with the newer employees, as far as motivation is concerned, is honesty. We can't play any games with this group—just as we shouldn't play games with any of our employees. The new employees have the capacity to be open and frank, and we aren't used to that. When we first encounter such frankness, we nearly always say or do the wrong thing, thus discouraging the employee from opening up to us again. We can overcome this by being open with the employee and telling him or her how we feel, even if in the beginning it embarrasses us or makes us feel uncomfortable. Knowing that the younger employees will respond to motivators just like everyone else will help us greatly in dealing with them. We just have to be sure that they know we're on their side in the matter and that what we're doing isn't intended to be all good for the organization and no good for them. Of course, just telling them won't convince them; we have to convince them by the results we get. If we say we're going to give them responsibility for a certain project but then decide we don't like the way they're doing it, or doubt that they're doing it correctly and start checking on them every few moments, we've lost whatever we hoped to gain in the way of motivating them. Further, we'll have a hard time even getting back to where we were when we started.

It isn't just a matter of playing by their rules; it's a matter of using their value system when we decide to motivate them. We must remember that they probably came to work suspicious of the organization and certainly with little love for it. If our initial effort at motivating them ends up showing that our concern wasn't really for them but to accomplish something for the organization, we'll confirm their suspicions, and *rightly so.* Whatever we do, we must avoid hypocrisy. They expect it, and if we aren't careful, they will see it even where it doesn't exist. No matter how much integrity we have when we start using the various means to motivation, we must do a lot of proving before they'll believe we have the workers' welfare in mind. It's worth the proving effort, though, because once we have convinced them that we will do things openly, that we do have a job to do for the organization, and that they will get as much consideration as we can give them (as long as the organization that's paying both our salaries doesn't get the bad end of the deal), then we'll begin to build a loyalty that will endure a lot of bad decisions and poor organizational policies. It's at this point that all the effort starts to pay off.

CONCLUSION

There are some things we know for sure about people of any age and any generation. We can use this information as long as we realize that it has to be used with some wisdom and care. Unfortunately, we don't know as much about how and when to use the information as we know about its existence. There are some ways of learning these things, too, however, so we have to be alert as we try them out. The newer workers respond to the same motivation, but our action usually must be different. Trying to find the key to which action to use at what time is our most difficult task; if we just throw up our hands in despair, we won't be successful at all. In fact, our employees will be so dissatisfied that they will be able to make our days pretty long and our lives pretty miserable. When we begin to experiment with motivating our employees and keep an open mind while we're doing it, we'll be pleasantly surprised at the results. Motivation will work, and it will work with any group of any age. We've got the tools to work with; we just need to learn how to use them well before they become rusty and unusable. *The results are well worth the effort.*

DISCUSSION QUESTIONS

1. What things are important to believe and accept before understanding motivation?

2. Define motivation.

3. List again several things we know for sure about people. These are important because they are the very things we use in motivational efforts.

4. The items in the preceding list are the tools to use in motivating employees. What must accompany these to avoid problems?

5. What is the most critical element in dealing with the newer employee as far as motivation is concerned?

Chapter nine

Delegation

Perhaps the most significant key to dealing with the new work force's desire to be a part of what is going on in the organization is the supervisor's ability to learn and practice good delegation. Today's work force generally wants to grow and develop and do consistently more responsible things. They have impatience that frustrates them when they aren't constantly moving up or into different areas. The beauty of delegation is that it allows us to let them see tangible evidence of things they are learning to do when they are seeking opportunities to be a part of any organization, whether it be business or personal. Delegation allows them to get involved in some decision making and problem solving. For that reason supervisors who become the most successful are the ones who learn the skill of delegation. But delegation requires a certain amount of finesse and skill, or it will be perceived by the work force as just another way of getting more work to do. In this chapter we talk about why we delegate, what we do and don't delegate, whom or whom not to delegate to, and some of the skills required in being successful at delegation.

THE PURPOSE OF DELEGATION

First let's notice some things delegation is not intended to accomplish, even though it does in fact accomplish some of these things. The purpose of delegation is not for the supervisor just to get rid of unwanted work. If the supervisor is doing things that are supposed to be a part of the supervisor's job but are so boring, routine, and monotonous that the supervisor decides that these would be good things to delegate, some serious drawbacks are going to appear. The purpose of delegation is also not just to challenge people—to find people who seem to be bored with what they are doing or who may be very good at what they are doing and give them a very challenging assignment just for the sake of giving them a challenge. There is nothing wrong with giving challenging assignments, of course, and if the delegation is given to the right person at the right time, then certainly challenge is going to result. Challenge is, however, a secondary benefit—not the primary reason for delegating. It is also not the purpose of delegation to appraise employees on existing jobs. There should be enough about the existing job for us to measure without having to delegate something that is not a routine part of that job. The existing job has standards and activities that are measurable and for which there are ample opportunities to observe the employee working either above, below, or at the standards. When we delegate something to someone, it involves work that is beyond the regular job. It is something that is not a part of what we expect of an employee day in and day out. Hence, it would be neither fair nor wise to use the delegation of other assignments as a means of appraising the person on the existing job.

If the purpose of the delegation is none of the things discussed thus far, what is the purpose? First of all, almost every action, activity, or job assignment we make that comes under the heading of delegation should primarily be done as a means of getting the work done at the lowest possible level of competency in the organization. We'll see later that that's the prime consideration in several other aspects. There are people in the organization who can perform a task that's presently being performed at a higher level. It is economical and very prudent, most of the time, to see that that job is done at the lowest level. It is also the purpose of delegation to develop people for larger or different jobs from the one they are now doing.

When we give an employee an assignment that is different from the one they have, even if it is not a more important job or even a more difficult job, it at least provides an opportunity to grow and develop in some area that they are not presently familiar with. This is especially valuable with the members of the work force of today, who are looking for a challenge and an opportunity to do something different. This allows them to develop certain skills that they may find interesting or useful, or to discover that they don't like a particular kind of work. Not only will they find out, but we'll also find out if they're good or bad in that kind of assignment. Another purpose of delegating is to relieve the supervisor of some of the jobs that could be done at a lower level of competency and to allow the supervisor to have more time for the managerial functions that often get overlooked. By delegating certain responsibilities or activities the supervisor can gain time for planning and managing the work and doing more of the paperwork that is burdensome but can only be done by the supervisor.

The purpose of delegation is to assess potential that employees may have for jobs other than their own. While the purpose is not to appraise them in their existing jobs, it does serve a very good means of looking at people as they try out jobs that are somewhat different from what they are presently doing. This give us a chance to look at them during a reasonably threat-free activity because they may not do this same job all the time. We should do this only under certain conditions, which we will discuss later, because we certainly don't want to base assessments of employees' potentials on how well they do a job for which they have not been trained. One final purpose is that delegation simply allows us to utilize to a near maximum the human resources in our organization. One of the interesting things about human resources is that they are the only resources that can get more valuable the more they're used. Almost every other resource uses itself up or becomes less valuable as it is used. People, however, ought to be more valuable today than they were yesterday, a year from now than they are today, and ten years from now than they are this year. Delegation gives us an opportunity to expand these resources and hence use them to better advantage.

TO WHOM DO WE DELEGATE?

Again we'll look at the negative side first—at people to whom we do *not* delegate. First, it is very important that you do not delegate additional responsibility, accountability, and authority to unsatisfactory performers. We don't want to reward people for incompetency, and in almost every case—if it is done correctly—delegation will be perceived as a reward or recognition of some kind. Sometimes supervisors will attempt to motivate an employee by giving him or her an assignment that is beyond the employee's own job, carries more authority, or puts the employee in the limelight. If this employee is a poor performer and is not doing as good a job as the other people are doing, it won't take long for strife to develop among those who feel that they should have had the recognition or the responsibility we gave to the poor performer. We also should not delegate to people who have demonstrated that they have a lack of ability in a particular area. If we've delegated a task to such people before without success, and if in the meantime they haven't done anything to improve themselves or to develop their talent or skills in that area, we should be very cautious about delegating the same task to them again. Not only will the job not get done as it should, but we will further erode the employees' self confidence by giving them the same task at which they have already failed once.

One point that is sometimes confusing is that we don't necessarily delegate to the most capable people. Delegation is a means of developing people—getting them trained to do jobs requiring greater responsibility or different skills—but if we continue to delegate to the person who already has the most skills, that person will simply get better and better while others do not become any more proficient at other tasks. Obviously we want the job done correctly, and if a person is particularly good at something and we see that that person may eventually take a job that will allow him or her to do that all the time, we would want to delegate to that person those tasks that exercise that capability. But generally speaking we do not delegate to the most capable person *just because* he or she is the most capable.

On a similar note, we do not delegate to the same person all the time. If we aren't careful we'll find ourselves delegating certain tasks to certain people, and other tasks to other people. Every time that particular task comes up we will just turn it over to the person who did it the last time. What we will have effectively done will be to make that task a part of the person's job responsibilities rather than letting it remain a matter of delegation. Again, if our purpose is training, developing, and assessing people and their potential in other jobs, we want to spread the delegation around to different employees in order to get a greater number of people trained and a better look at the capabilities of our people.

Now that we have seen the people to whom we do not delegate, how about those to whom we do? Well, first of all we delegate to those people who have shown some interest in growing and developing themselves. Sometimes employees will come to us and say, "I'd like to learn how to do that job over there." Or, "I'd like to do the job that you are doing now." If those people are satisfactory employees, have previously demonstrated a willingness to learn, and have accepted tasks and completed those tasks on time, there is perhaps no reason why we can't delegate to them. We certainly want to encourage the employees to grow and develop, and we ought to be excited about the prospect of someone coming to us wanting to expand his or her knowledge level and ability to help the organization. So we try to delegate to those people who express an interest in particular jobs or in growing in certain areas.

Next, we delegate to those who have done well in smaller areas of responsibilities that are perhaps similar to the ones that we are thinking about delegating at this time. We want to continue to stretch our people, but we don't want to challenge them beyond their abilities. We want to challenge our people also in new areas, so we don't necessarily want to just keep giving them bigger and bigger tasks that build on the same activity that they have been doing before. However, as we said before, if we foresee that an employee eventually will move into a job in which he or she will be doing a certain task all the time with greater responsibilities and greater requirements, we can gradually ease him or her into this by increasing the amount of responsibility we delegate. On the other hand, if we are still assessing potential and we find that an employee did very well in a particular activity when we delegated it, we can feel free to enlarge the amount of delegation in another area or perhaps even in a smaller area in some other field. Along these same lines we should point out that we delegate to those people we expect to promote someday. Since this is a good way of assessing people's potential, we can delegate to people to find out just how soon we can promote them and in what areas they seem to have the most competency.

We want to delegate to those people that we wish to assess in certain areas. If we want to find out how good their letter writing has become or how good they are at running meetings or how good they are at doing reports or handling certain types of employee problems, then we can delegate those particular assignments to them. It should be noted, however, that if we are going to rate them or evaluate them in some way, they ought to know ahead of time what our intent is. They ought to know that we are going to see how well they can handle a certain situation—how well they write those letters, conduct this meeting, or handle this particular employee situation. They should know ahead of time what we are looking for and what we expect of them, and that we will in fact use this information in some way as a means of assessing their potential for even greater assignments.

Finally, we delegate to those people who might have tried the same task before and failed. This is especially true of members of today's work force, who are not very much in the habit of failing and are not very pleased with a failing record. This may sound like a contradiction, but the truth is that we will delegate to those people who have failed providing they have used their previous failure as a means of learning something. If they have taken the time to ask questions or experiment or work on activities on their own, perhaps even taken some outside training to improve their ability, then by all means they deserve another chance to try to accomplish that same task. Whereas we would not want to delegate to someone who has demonstrated a lack of ability and also a lack of interest in doing a particular kind of work, we would want very much to delegate to someone who showed an interest and wanted to overcome a previous failure. It should be pointed out to them, of course, that there is a possibility of failure, but if we have reasonably good evidence that they can succeed we ought to let them try. We use delegation as a developmental tool. The previous failure should have allowed us to provide very effective training and helped them a great deal toward becoming better in this particular work assignment.

WHAT DO WE DELEGATE?

As usual let's start off with the things that we do not delegate before we get to the things that we should or can delegate. First, we obviously should not delegate things that require our authority or our position or our job level to accomplish. If part of the activity requires dealing with someone at our own level, we probably would not want to delegate it because it would lose some of its authority. Also, if we are giving rewards to people, are going to discuss a promotion or job change, or are doing a performance appraisal or some other kind of counseling, we would not want to delegate. While these do not all necessarily require a certain level of authority, it may be that there is some prestige or recognition for other employees involved. If that's the case, then in all fairness to the employees involved we should do it ourselves instead of delegating it to someone at a lower level. Whenever we are handing out recognition or discussing job changes we ought to put all the prestige of our position into it. This would be a dangerous area to do any delegation.

At the other end of the spectrum, so to speak, we do not want to delegate those things that pertain to any kind of employee discipline involving a violation of a work rule or any other kind of unsatisfactory performance on the part of an employee. We do not want to lose the impact of the authority inherent in our position by delegating such a task to someone else.

We would not want to delegate anything that might jeopardize employees because of safety considerations or possible consequences of violating rules imposed by an outside organization. If there is a possibility of injury to an employee or damage to equipment due to the employee's ignorance of, or lack of, responsibility and accountability for the safety rules, then we should avoid delegating at that time. Overall, if the government has imposed on certain activities or jobs rules that for proper decision making require our level of expertise or authority, then we should not delegate decisions about that job to someone else. Usually in such cases, as we have seen in earlier chapters, there are serious consequences for the violation of some rules and regulations, and it is not fair to employees if we rid ourselves of responsibility by delegating these to someone else. On the other hand, it might not be fair to us if we delegate the activity to someone who unintentionally violates a rule or regulation, because we alone will be answerable to the regulating agency.

Now let's look at some things that we *should* delegate. First, we should delegate only those things that we have the authority to delegate. If something has been assigned to us and we are expected to carry it out and will be responsible for it, then by all means we ought to keep it. If we do want to delegate such an activity, we should get clearance from the person who delegated it to us—or perhaps request that the activity be assigned to us—so we can delegate it with clear conscience and with organizational approval. Also remember that we delegate only what is normally a part of our job and not a part of the employees' job. If we give somebody something to do that they are already supposed to be doing, it is not delegation. Since delegation of an assignment does not mean that the person delegated to will do that job from that point on, we delegate a part of our work or a part of a job that we want to let the person work on or learn or get some experience in.

When we delegate a task to an individual, we should be careful not to violate established work rules and to avoid setting a precedent in our department or the organization—allowing someone at a different level to do a job that has previously been reserved for our level. If we feel that it's important that we delegate a particular temporary assignment to a particular person, and suspect that this might set a precedent, we would do well to take whatever steps are necessary to clear this trial or temporary assignment with personnel, the union, or anyone that might be involved.

It is not enough merely to delegate those things that will offer the employee a chance to develop new skills and improve on existing ones. We ought to have specific skills in mind when we delegate. We ought to understand the skills required to complete the job, know the standards we expect, and communicate these to the employee. If we are trying to help the employee improve on a specific skill, we should sit down with the employee and say, "This is the specific area of improvement we're looking for." As mentioned previously, we should also point out that when the activity is over we will sit down with the employee and discuss how much he or she improved in the designated area and what might be done to improve even more in the future.

STEPS IN DELEGATION

We've talked about what and to whom we delegate, but now let's take a look at the steps in successful delegation. First, we determine to whom we want to delegate, what can and should be delegated, and proceed from there. (It should be noted here though that we don't *have* to delegate. However, as we look back over the purposes of delegation it is obvious that we're better off if we do delegate as much as possible as often as possible.) When we decide that we are going to delegate *we ought to know the purpose* for that delegation. For example:

1. We need to get a certain job done at a lower level to free ourselves for other work and we know that the competency exists at that level, then that's our purpose.

2. We have someone who is obviously prepared for a greater challenge and more responsibility, and either shows good aptitude for or is already proficient in a particular job, then that's the purpose.

3. We feel that an employee needs to develop a certain skill for an upcoming assignment, then that's our purpose for delegating at this point.

Before we delegate, we need to look at the performance records of the people we are considering, to determine primarily two things: First, we need to know the amount of experience or knowledge a person has with regard to the particular task we are going to delegate and the degree of motivation a person has—not only for this assignment, but for similar assignments in the past. If the experience and knowledge is low, we know we are going to have to do some training, and we're going to have to set some milestones along the way to see whether or not each job is being completed when it should be. Not because of the lack of motivation, but because the individual doesn't have the experience to know when the deadlines should be falling and what should be finished at a particular time. If the experience or knowledge level is high then obviously we don't need to do the training and we probably don't need to set checkpoints to see how the project is going. On the other hand, if the motivation is high we know we won't have to do much selling in the beginning in order to motivate the person to give their full attention to the project. We won't have to do much tracking along the way because the person will come to us if there is a problem; however, if the individual has not shown much success at meeting deadlines or settling in to work on a project as soon as it is assigned, then motivation might be a problem, and we'll have to do some selling in the beginning and probably quite a bit of tracking along the way.

The worst possible thing we could do—whatever our style might be—would be to use the same approach on all people. We must be flexible. If a person has a bad track record with regard to completion, getting started, or detail work, and we want the task finished by this person at a particular time, then we're going to have to do the checking required to see if progress is being made—even if the person dislikes us looking over his or her shoulder. We have the past history to fall back on to show the reason we're doing it this way. On the other hand, if the employee has a track record of being motivated and knowledgeable in the area we are talking about, probably the worst thing we could do would be to track and follow up and look over his or her shoulder.

Before we turn an employee loose on a job, we need to make it clear what our expectations are and how we will operate in this particular task as he or she works on it. For example, if we are going to track, if there are deadlines, or if we're going to let the individual come to us rather than our going to him or her, we should explain these points in advance. In addition we want to let the person know how we're going to measure performance at the end of an assignment, and make it clear just how much assistance we will be able to give on the project. We want to let the person know when we will be available and how much time—if any—we're willing to put into helping to finish up or get the project caught up. Finally we need to explain the degree of accountability there is going to be in this project. If there is going to be credit or recognition given, this ought to be pointed out. At the same time, if the person is going to be held accountable for errors, mistakes, and bad decisions, this should be made perfectly clear in advance.

In the next step, when the project is over, we follow up and evaluate how well the project has been handled. We will need a record of the assistance that we have given, deadlines that have been met, milestones that have been crossed, places where we have had to do additional training and where we have had to step in and solve difficult or unusual problems. When it's all over, we take a look at the project and the action that was taken on the project, and we measure all of these against the standards that we set in the beginning. Whatever the final outcome, we should be sure to give the reward or recognition that is merited and additional training or counseling that might be needed to make sure future projects are done properly.

If the project was intended to be a learning experience or developmental activity, we need to make sure that we spend the time with the individual making it just that—sitting down with him or her and letting him or her know beyond a shadow of a doubt just exactly how we feel about what has been accomplished. If further training is needed, we will explain how this training can be arranged. If the individual needs to learn to work in some areas on his or her own, we need to point that out as well. We may want to make an entry in the personnel records indicating that this assignment was done and how well it was done. Delegation should not be taken lightly. It is a serious project and we want to approach it in as formal a way as possible not only to ensure that a good product results, but that the individual will be better for having done the assignment. Today's work force expects this. They don't always get it. It's pretty distressing for them not to know what they're supposed to be doing, not to know how well they are doing, and then finding out only much later—if at all—that they were either good or bad in the eyes of the supervisor.

CONCLUSION

We have found that there are some good reasons for delegating. While we don't have to delegate, we very much need to consider delegating those tasks that can be done by the people under us. Today's work force is impatient enough and often ambitious enough to keep us on our toes in learning how to delegate effectively. Delegation is perhaps the best tool we have for getting these employees involved in what's going on in the organization. But like many tools it takes skill to use, and we need to learn those skills. Perhaps the most exciting thing that will come out of it is that we'll have time enough to do our job better and take on things that are delegated to us by our bosses!

QUESTIONS FOR DISCUSSION

1. Think of two or three specific supervisors that we've had in the past and list the characteristics of each

as far as delegation is concerned. Did they have a specific style of delegating? Did they delegate the same to everybody? Did they show favorites? Did they use delegation as a developmental tool?

2. Think about a specific task that needs to be delegated to a specific person. Decide which style of delegating would best be suited for this particular person doing this particular assignment. In this case use only the two considerations that we discussed: experience or knowledge and motivation or lack of it.

3. List the advantages of delegating tasks to subordinates—especially the ones mentioned in this chapter. See how many others can be named.

4. Now name as many disadvantages or hazards to delegation as you can think of. Put your list beside the list from question 3 and see which one outweighs the other.

5. Explain why so many bosses fail to delegate many of the tasks that could be done as well or nearly as well by subordinates.

part four

Positive Supervision

Chapter ten

Handling Time

"I don't have time!" How many times have we heard that phrase? How many times have we used it ourselves? Usually, when one starts to talk about "time management," somebody chimes in with the old expression, "Everybody has the same amount of time: twenty-four hours a day." As true as this is, it isn't very comforting to a harried supervisor who is behind in every phase of the work, needs more time than is available to get the job done, and works all the available hours in the day—and night! Yet we all recognize that some people seem to have more time than others. Some get more done than others in the same amount of time, and even very busy people often can take on more work responsibility and additional assignments and still get the job done. Others have less to do and yet can never catch up and finish anything on time. What's the secret? Are some smarter, faster, or better organized? The solution is simple to explain but difficult to accomplish. It's called time management. Few supervisors are good at it or have the patience to do it well, even after they understand it.

This is one subject in which we could all take a lesson

"We got the boss a book on time management last year, but he hasn't had time to read it yet."

from the new generation coming into the work force. These younger people grew up in busy times and thus were always doing something; even though they perhaps have learned to slow down and smell the roses occasionally, they do get things done. They can take on several jobs, get interested in many hobbies, travel great distances in a small amount of time, and still survive. They've learned some things about using their time. Often they are involved in so many things that we go wild trying to stay with them, but they get much more done in twenty-four hours than many of us do. It may well be that we can learn from them and in turn teach them some things about how to make their ability pay off in greater dividends for them. In this chapter, we'll find out what time is, how we can manage the time we have, how we can get it to work for us, and how we can quit being a slave to it. We'll also see how to do our daily planning to get the most out of available time.

WHAT IS TIME?

Time is difficult to define, but for our purposes let's simplify it by saying that it measures the period between two instants. Perhaps we could say that it is the interval between two events; but the events themselves take time, so we will just conclude that time is what goes between any given instant and another instant. This definition suits our purposes because it suggests a *beginning* and an *ending*. To see the importance of this, note that it is one thing to ask, "What time is it?" but quite another to ask, "How much time will this take?" One is a designation of an instant, whereas the other is a way of specifying a period between two instants, that is, the *starting* and the *stopping* points. We also need to come to an understanding of the expression "managing time." When we say we're going to manage time, we're saying that we plan to manage the interval between two instants, but we'll see that this may not be the right way to express what we plan to do. To understand managing time, we need to notice the following:

1. It is easy to quantify time. Time can be measured accurately to as small a unit as we choose. The measurements are easy to define and readily known by everyone. We speak of a second or a minute or an hour, day, week, month, or year; the measurement is exact in every case. If you say, "This will take two weeks," everyone knows exactly how much time you're talking about.

2. Time never stands still. Like a falling rock or water running down hill, time passes by without stopping. When you tell somebody to wait a minute, they will not stop the clock. Time will go on, and that particular minute will never be around again.

3. The speed of time is constant for everyone. Like distance from one point to another, the period from one instant to another is the same for everyone alive at the two instants. For the small child waiting for a birthday party, time may seem to go by very slowly; for the aged person concerned with the little life remaining, time seems to fly. To the boy on his way to meet his girlfriend, it seems to take forever to get there; to the girl who is trying to get herself as well dressed and attractive as possible, it seems that the clock speeds and that she will not have enough time to get the job done.

4. Time cannot be regulated. Since we can neither stop nor speed up the clock to suit our desires and fears, we cannot regulate how fast it goes. We cannot influence it in any way; hence, we cannot actually "manage" it. More properly, we can only manage our *use* of the *fixed amount* of time we have available.

It is advantageous to know all these things about time, simply to make it possible to get control of ourselves during the time we have to do whatever projects or assignments we have to do. In many ways, we cannot deal with time very effectively because we don't understand it. It is much like a complex machine in the hands of an inexperienced operator. The machine may run because it is turned on, but getting it to perform up to its full potential is quite difficult for the inexperienced operator. For example, new supervisors are usually accustomed to having their time allocated so that they need to make few decisions about time use. However, they soon find that the responsibility has shifted so that now decisions about time are required for both them and their employees. It's a challenge that most find difficult to handle.

IS TIME MONEY?

According to a very shop-worn expression, time is money. It's not a very meaningful expression, but it sounds good. Supervisors frequently use it when they see employees not doing anything, suggesting that not doing anything wastes money and that being busy saves money. Of course, that's true only if the time in which we aren't doing anything could be used along with raw material and skill to produce something worthwhile and usable. It's also true only if we use the "saved" time properly. So time is not money, though there is certainly a relationship between time and money. We learn a better lesson about money and time from the analogy that results when we *compare* time and money. Let's notice some things about this.

First, time can be budgeted. Just as with money, we can set aside a period of time to accomplish certain things; as is also the case with money, we may end up having either too much or too little time when we start to use it for the project. We can also budget time by cutting out certain things that we decide we don't have enough time for. If we see that time is going to be short, we leave certain things out of our time budget; if we see that we will have some spare time, we add some things to the budget.

Next, we can deal only with the time we have, so *we must know how much we have.* This is the downfall of most people who run out of time, never have enough time, or are always late. They don't know how much time they have, and they don't know where their time is going. When we are planning for the use of a certain period of time, we need to determine first where the time is coming from. Will we have to take it from some other part of the time budget? Is there time to spare because we don't have anything planned? Are we kidding ourselves into thinking that the time will be there, even though we aren't certain where it will come from? Maybe we're just burying our heads in the sand, not thinking that far ahead and going on with a planned activity without even testing the time budget to see if it will accommodate our time need. Finally, we have to ask ourselves if we can give up something else or get it done more quickly to make room for the project we are now trying to fit into our budget. This is the point at which we decide if the tradeoff is worth it; it gets us to the manner in which time decisions are made—deciding exactly what we want to do with out time, in order of priority.

We have to set priorities for our time, just as we do for our money. Since we rarely have as much money as we can spend, we make decisions on the basis of priorities. We decide what is more or less important to us and what we are willing to give up to be able to have the more important. We decide which tradeoffs we're williing to make— what we're willing to give to get something else. The same procedure will help us do the best job of using our time. We do it that way anyway, but we just don't admit it. It is usually not true when we say that we don't have time for something. What we really mean is that the thing doesn't yet have a high enough priority to make us give up something else to do it. "I'd like to write a book," somebody says, "but I just don't have the time." Remember that those who write books have only the same amount of time as those who don't write books. Those who don't may watch television twenty hours a week, go to ball games, jog a couple of miles a day, or take a vacation on the beach. Most people with anything to say can write a book in the time that other people use in a year jogging, watching television, or going to sports events. The answer comes back, "But these things are important to my health!" That's not the issue, is it? The issue is whether jogging, television, or sports has a higher priority than writing a book. It does if you do it instead of writing the book. It's not a question of what is good or bad for us or what is a service to our families or to the world in general; it's just a matter of what's high on our lists of priorities. Some people say they don't have time for exercise because of their jobs, but when bad health and the doctor's orders change their priorities, they suddenly find time for exercise.

Another way to compare time with money is to measure the amount we spend on certain items to determine our budget for the next time period. Nobody can set a financial budget that works unless they first find out where their money is going, right down to the nickels and dimes. The only way to do this is to keep track of every cent spent over a given period until we begin to see a pattern develop. Most people who have done this have been surprised at where their money really went—surprised at how much they spent each week for candy, cigarettes, or taxis, for example. They often find that the little things amount to a large part of their expenditures. So it is with time use. If we can bring ourselves to keep up with our day-to-day activities until we begin to see a pattern of how much time we spend doing various things, we are usually surprised that inconsequential things use much of our time. We spend hours each year just sitting at traffic lights or stop signs; we devote days to eating; we spend weeks watching television. Surprisingly, we never even think about those things as something we have to budget. We know about the working hours, the sleeping hours, and the meeting hours, but we may not realize how many hours we spend talking on the telephone or lingering over a cup of coffee. Until we find out where all this time is going, we'll never be able to set a time budget. Remember, though, it isn't very exciting to try to find our time usage over a certain period in, say, fifteen-minute intervals. Just as it's hard to keep up with the nickels and dimes, it's hard to keep up with the ten- and fifteen-minute periods of our lives.

SLAVERY TO TIME

We've already seen that it's not really possible to "manage" time, since time is constant and always moves at the same rate. However, time can surely manage us. We can become slaves to it, and many of us allow our lives and activities to be almost dominated by time. We become *reverse clock-watchers.* Instead of watching the clock so we'll know when to *leave* work, go on our own time and relax, we watch the clock to make certain we're getting all the work done we can. If we see that time is going by "fast," we panic, trying to work harder to get more done before time "runs out." When something interferes with our work and we "get behind" in time, we drive ourselves to try to "catch up" on time. When these things happen, time is managing us.

Good use of time requires good planning, but good planning also requires taking time. If we have become a slave to time, one of the first things to go is the time we should be spending planning. We "just don't have the time" to do a good job of planning; hence, we end up doing a poor job of using the time we have available. This puts us further behind, and we take less time to evaluate where we are and where we should be spending our time most profitably, and thus we get even further behind. As a result, we become frustrated and spend too much time after hours, either at work or at home, thinking about it and feeling guilty because we aren't trying to catch up. For many, life is simply one long, endless "rat race." There are few such conditions that could not have been helped in the beginning by better planning, and perhaps even fewer that cannot be helped now with *better time use.*

DOING THE UNNECESSARY

When we begin to analyze how we spend our time, one of the first things we see is that we do many things that could have been left undone or that could have been done at some other time. Planning our time well requires that we determine what we should and should not be doing. If we choose what to do on the basis of what we like or want to do, rather than on what we ought or need to do, we'll find ourselves doing many unnecessary things and leaving many necessary things undone. We often talk of "procrastination," but if we examine this behavior closely, we'll often find that procrastinators haven't stopped *doing things* but rather that they've been busy *doing the wrong things.* They postpone the essentials because they either dread getting started, aren't very excited about that particular job, or maybe even think that what they are doing is important enough to delay the other activity. Supervisors often do the "wrong things" by failing to delegate tasks to those who are supposed to be doing them. Because we know how to handle the tasks or get a lot of satisfaction from doing something with our hands, we hate to delegate them. This is even more noticeable when our alternative is doing something we don't like or doing something less "tangible," such as making an unpleasant decision.

Anytime we find ourselves doing the wrong jobs, losing time doing them, or failing to delegate, there is at least a strong indication that we haven't planned our time use very well. When we fail to plan, we tend to start our day's work with the first thing that comes along, instead of the most important thing. If, as we walk into the office or plant, somebody asks for an address and telephone number, we haven't started the day on our own schedule. It may take us several minutes to find the information and because it's hard to find, we may even feel good when we do so. We get a feeling of accomplishment and may even say to ourselves that, "things are getting off to a good start." Actually, things are going to be pretty bad if we spend the rest of the day working for somebody else. We come in, pick up a piece of paper, answer the phone and respond to somebody's question, and are off and running in what we'll probably describe later as a "hectic day." We will also say that it doesn't make any difference if we plan our time because nobody else lets us keep to the plan. Through poor time use we've made our own days hectic, yet we want to blame others.

We started out by saying that we could learn some things from the newer generation about getting things done. As we look at them, we see that they do, in fact, often accomplish many, many things once they set their minds to doing them. Being told that there isn't enough time (just like being told that there isn't enough money) sounds ridiculous to them. They will appear to have overcommitted themselves, taking on much more than they should be able to get done, and yet they always seem to be able to get these things done. If we watch them closely, we'll see that there are several reasons for their success. First, when they make a commitment to themselves and to others, they work hard at keeping it. Next, they approach their work thinking, "It can be done" rather than, "It can't be done in this amount of time." Third, they may not even think of time as one of the elements to be considered in getting work done. They simply decide to do something and set about doing it without worrying about how much time they have or whether they'll have enough. Next, they have the ability to do more than one thing at a time. They don't let things bother them to the extent that they can't do one thing because they're too busy worrying about something else. Finally, they are willing to put in the time necessary to accomplish the things they have committed themselves to. It doesn't matter much to them if they have to put in late hours or get up early if that's what it takes to meet their goals.

Their approach has several problem areas, which we need to discuss. One is that they are not likely to make a commitment and spend time on things that have to do with the job, unless it is something in which they have an interest or that they have thought about themselves. The kinds of commitments we've been talking about usually have to do with personal business or pleasure, hobbies, or activities with family and friends. One reason why they often don't have this commitment on the job is that they see their efforts at getting things done thwarted by red tape and others' excuses that they just "can't get things done that fast around here." They see so many people seemingly trying *not* to get things done that they just don't put in much energy hurrying to accomplish more than they must. Another problem with what they are doing is that in the long run we have to consider how much time things will take, and we can't go through our entire lives getting things done by sleeping less and eating at odd intervals. If we do, we're letting time manage us. There is much to be said for the fact that the younger working people can generate energy toward accomplishing goals and that they can handle more than one thing at a time, but in the long run it would be more practical for them if they could do a better job of planning their activities by considering time rather than just ignoring it. Once we've mastered time usage ourselves, we can help them do so. Some good counseling, based on our desire to help them control their time use, will pay off for the job and for them. Just letting them know that we're amazed at what they can get done when they set their goals will show that we are aware of their capabilities. That alone will surprise them; they probably think we have never noticed.

USING OUR TIME WELL

So far in comparing time and money, we have seen that we can't manage time but that it can manage us. We have also noted some of the things about setting priorities so that our time will be well spent. Now we need to look at some specific ways to make better use of the time we have and the time we plan to have. First—and this takes us back to what has already been said several times—we need to know how much time we have. We find this out only through a skillful analysis of how much we want to do and how long it will take us to do the things already planned, plus the things we want to work into our schedule. If we do a poor job here, everything else is going to suffer.

Next, we must schedule time for contingencies. We may do a good job of setting our priorities, only to see them get changed. The beauty of knowing our priorities is that when something comes up, we can make adjustments by looking at our priorities rather than just flying off after some other activity. The contingency may be of our own making—we see that something else more important has come up—or it may be imposed on us by somebody else—the boss has rearranged our priorities. In either case we know that these things happen, and we must be sure to give ourselves the luxury of flexibility in time use to avoid panic or despair when they do.

Perhaps the most significant improvement we can make in planning time is to start doing our planning on a psychological basis. If we think about it, we'll see that much of our anguish about time use comes from the psychological problems of worrying about having too little time or failing to get the job done at all and then feeling we've wasted time. We dread doing some things we need to accomplish, so we find ourselves procrastinating. We may find ourselves facing a hard job or a long assignment at a time of day when we aren't ready to do it; or just as we finish a difficult project and are ready to celebrate, we see that the next thing coming up is something else equally difficult, and hence no reward. All these are psychological as well as time management problems.

To avoid some of these problems, we look at ourselves and decide just how many difficult projects we can take at any given time. Then, when we plan something that uses up this tolerance, we schedule a rewarding project right after it. As we'll see later, we may even plan our schedule with a break *just to do nothing.* Some of the things we have to do in every workday are so routine that we do little thinking and no worrying about them. These are the things to schedule after a difficult task. Many people do their best work in the morning, so they prefer to schedule their challenging jobs then. Others know that they don't get wound up until afternoon, so they do the little, routine jobs in the morning and save the larger, more complicated ones until the afternoon. Each person will have to find his or her own best time for such activities, and that time will vary a little with each person. If we see that a certain project or activity is likely to give little satisfaction or could even end in failure, we should plan some short, sure successes to come immediately on the heels of the less certain one. In this way we won't dwell too long on our failures and will be in the midst of a pretty sure success before we can let it get us down too much.

USING A PRIORITY LIST

We've seen that things to be done should be put on a priority list, with the important things first and the lesser things later. A good way to make such a list is to look at the things we've decided we'd like to do and then make a statement about each one. If there is something that must be done, we rank it that way under "must." To determine whether things belong under this heading, we ask ourselves some questions about them. "What would happen if we didn't do it now? What would happen if we didn't do it at all? What would happen if somebody else had to do it? Should somebody else be doing it anyway?" The answers to these questions will yield all the data we need to decide where the activity belongs on our list.

Next, we rank items that are "near-musts." These are the

ones that we can get by without doing, even though the results aren't very satisfying when we leave them undone. They're borderline cases, and only judgment can tell us for sure where to put them.

The next ranking is "nice." These are things that are likely to get us into trouble, since they almost always have some emotional or prejudicial pull behind them. They are things that we like to do or want to do to impress somebody but can't really justify as being musts or near-musts. As with the near-musts, we have to use judgment in deciding about them. We can star them as a reminder that one of them can serve as a reward when we've accomplished a very difficult and time-consuming task. It doesn't matter that it is something we don't have to do; we've earned the right to "squander" a little time on something we'd like very much to do. As long as the task doesn't take too long or actually keep us from getting to something that must be done, it's a fitting reward.

Finally, there are items that would be nice to do but really don't need to be done. We don't particularly want to do them, and even though they have lost their urgency, we've carried them along because at one time they seemed more important than they do now. We list them under "nice," then scratch them out altogether. If they ever get important, they'll come back up without our having to refer to them; if we run out of time and need something to do, other things will be more important. As long as we keep them on the list of things to do, they'll just worry us and serve to "psych us down" when we think we're overloaded. Getting rid of them will give us a lift, so it's worth it for what we can gain from this effort.

Now let's see how to use the priority list. It's pretty easy: We schedule the musts and near-musts in the psychological order we talked about and save the "nice" list for some other time. As we've seen, we use it to reward ourselves or to fill in the times when we can't start on the next "must" because we're waiting for something or somebody. Most people like to do the nice things too often, so we have to practice some real discipline to keep them from getting out of hand. If we've clearly marked them on our list or in our minds in the nice category rather than in the must or near-must category, we won't have to worry about their getting too high on the priority list.

LIVING WITH INTERRUPTIONS

When we hear ourselves telling somebody, "I could get a lot more done if it weren't for all the interruptions," we are listening to ourselves making a bad mistake about how people get things done. People who accomplish things within time limits don't do it because they never have interruptions; they do it by living with their interruptions and learning how to control them. First, we have to admit that life is full of interruptions and that we can't go off and hide to get our job done. On occasion a little peace and quiet might help us get our thoughts together and our work done; however, if we can't learn to get work done in an environment where people come in unscheduled and telephones ring with calls we hadn't planned, we can never hope to be successful in today's work world. One of the advantages the younger employees have is that they seem to thrive on chaos, noise, and interruptions. Many older supervisors came from a world of concentration in very sedate circumstances and find themselves unable to deal with the frustrations of noise and interruptions.

It's easy enough to say that we have to be able to live with interruptions, but how do we do it? Simply enough, if we can develop some patterns of handling them. We've already finished part of the job, because most of us have reached the point where we at least admit that they do and will continue to exist. That's the first step in handling the problem. Next, we must decide if we're actually *encouraging* the interruptions. Without realizing it, we may be bringing much of the grief on ourselves, especially with people coming in or calling us. Why do they come in? Why do they keep calling us? Are the same people doing the interrupting? Once we begin to analyze the situation, we soon see that there are some good reasons for the interruptions. We may find that when people come in, we drop everything and try our best to help, thinking that if we help, they'll get out of our hair more quickly. What actually happens, of course, is that they get the feeling that we not only don't mind the interruption, but also may have been glad for the opportunity to help. Even if this isn't the case, we have at least made it a rewarding experience for them to come to us; this means they'll most likely come back again when they need help. The solution is to make this a less rewarding experience, still doing the part of our job that says we should offer certain kinds of help to certain people.

Unless a standard of our jobs says that anyone who comes along gets first choice of our time before we do anything on our own, we can set some standards of our own. If we stop our work for somebody who comes in or asks us to do something that interrupts what we have to do, we're saying that what *they* want is more important than what *we* are doing. To make matters worse, we're also saying this to them, thus they don't feel so bad about the interruption. We simply have to make it less convenient and less satisfying for them to use our valuable time. We don't do this by being rude or impolite or by refusing to help; rather, we do it by pointing out that we'll be glad to help as soon as it's convenient for us to take time from the important things we're doing. We offer to call them, or we set a time when we estimate we'll be free. We make it obvious that we are willing to help by pointing out that we will have more time then and can give them more attention.

The same is true for those who call us when we're not expecting it and want to get something that will take away from our own activities. It is an interesting phenomenon that if people think we're busy they will usually try to make an appointment when they want to discuss something with us *in person.* But when it comes to the telephone, they don't follow this rule. They call unannounced and expect us to accept them and their problem. We should realize what's happening and treat the interruption accordingly. We never want to appear uninterested in helping people, but we must let them know that we, too, have problems and that we aren't just sitting around waiting for somebody to call and give us something to do. If we help them every time they call, we give them this impression; we deserve such interruptions. If we can point out to them that we have something to do and will help them as soon as we take care of it, they'll soon know that they can't just interrupt us and get immediate action. Even if we delay them only for a short while, the result will be to show that we have some priorities and that we are controlling the way our time is used. The first time we do this it may take more time than if we were just to go ahead and handle the problem for them; but the lesson we give is worth it, and it will buy us a lot of time in the long run.

CONSCIOUS BUT NOT CONSCIENCE-STRICKEN

At times we won't do a very good job of planning our time use. We'll mess up, run over, miss deadlines, cause others to wait, leave some things undone, and generally wonder how we could botch things up so badly. It is at these times that we most need to have the PMA we talked about earlier: the positive mental attitude toward how we are going to live with these mistakes. We ought always to be conscious of where our time is going and what is happening to keep it from being used properly, but *without buckling to slavery*. We must be able to say, "Whew, I really blew that one! I misjudged the time completely and things were completely haywire. I've got to see that it doesn't happen again, if I can prevent it." Then we go on to the next assignment, having learned from our mistakes. It doesn't mean that we don't care about time; it just means that we realize that, after we've done our best, sometimes we'll still fail, and worrying about failures won't take them away. What will help, though, is studying the situation (not brooding over it) to see what we might learn about preventing a similar occurrence the next time we have to deal with something similar. We must sell ourselves on the idea that we're doing a lot more things right than wrong; as long as that's the case, we are doing a fine job of supervising. This isn't a coverup; *it's realism*.

Earlier we said that sometimes we should reward ourselves by *planning* to do nothing. Perhaps this is one of the most difficult elements in learning how to use time. We just can't bring ourselves to be inactive and still feel that we're accomplishing anything. Most of our training, even from childhood, has been that idleness is bad, almost unethical and immoral. When we look at idleness more closely, we see that it's virtually impossible to be *completely* idle, both mentally and physically. The idea behind the saying that "idle hands are the devil's workshop" is that when we are idle physically, we begin to use our minds more and are likely to be thinking the "wrong" thoughts. In the world of work, however, we *need* time to think and meditate about things around us. Most people are caught up in a very busy life, both on and off the job, and rarely take time to stop and consider where they've been or where they're going. Surveys show that many people, even in positions of authority, find it difficult to take just a few minutes to plan their activities for the day. Everything we know about planning tells us that it saves much more time than it takes, yet we aren't able to find that initial time to do our planning well.

Beyond just finding time to plan, we need to plan some time in which we don't do anything and don't do it on purpose. That is, time in which we don't plan to reach some goal. A recent song suggests that we need to "stop and smell the roses," and that's the idea. When we've finished a rather difficult task and want to enjoy that accomplishment, we should do so by going for a cup of coffee, looking out the window, or reading a magazine article about something not completely related to the job. The important thing is that we should do it as a part of the job, and not as something to sneak into the work schedule and feel guilty about. It's good for mental health, and it will help us undertake the next task with a little more vigor.

SETTING A WRITTEN SCHEDULE

Many people like to have some kind of written list of activities so they will know what's to be done. This is an excellent idea, and it is where we are headed when we make up lists of priorities. Of course, there are some additional advantages to this. At the end of the day we can see what we've done, and if we date the worksheets each day we can use them as a record of our activities. If we use "highlight" pens to cross the items off, we can still see them. Many like to make a broad sweep through the accomplished tasks for the moral and psychological lift it gives them, and there is much to be said for this approach.

There are many different ways to make up a work list. We can sit down in the morning, or even the night before, and list all the things we have to do in random order as we think of them. As we go down the list, we may choose to make some kind of mark to set priorities; maybe we just number the items in the order we think they should be handled. Another approach is to put stars or exclamation marks by the more urgent items. After we've listed everything we can think of that has to be done that day, we can redo the list, ranking the items by time of day or by importance. Nearly everyone who uses such a system realizes that it is impossible to finish every item on the list every day.

If there is ever time to think in a positive way, this is it. We must train ourselves to *see* all the things we've finished, not the things we still have to do. If there were ten items and we did seven, we must be able to look at the seven and realize that we got 70 percent of the items finished, not that we still had 30 percent of the list left. The items left on the sheet will still be there tomorrow, and they form the beginning of a new list. If some item continues to show up day after day, chances are pretty good that it isn't a high-priority item. After a couple of days of this, we should drop it and wait for it to get to be a higher-priority item. If it's important, we won't forget it; if it's not important, we ought to forget it!

CONCLUSION

Of course, there is much that we haven't said about time management. Time use is difficult to handle and hard to learn to handle well. However, it can be learned, and while we're learning it, we may have to suffer as we do when we're trying to learn to function under a monetary budget. There are those who become experts at using time, making every minute count and knowing where every minute goes.

They may even make others miserable with their constant clock-watching; when we don't conform to their idea of good time management, they might become very distressed with us. If they are happy in this role, then perhaps we should leave them alone to their joyous world of clocks, watches, and timetables. Not many of us can get this far in time use, if indeed we even want to. A better approach is to be a little more casual about it, to get control of ourselves and our time use gradually. We can do this step by step, finding out where our time is going, developing a habit of looking at priorities rather than seeing if we have time for something, developing an awareness of time and how we use it, planning what we do, trying to stick with the plan, and reviewing what happened to our time to see if we can do better in the future. Above all, we should work toward making time a valuable tool, rather than letting ourselves become slaves to it.

DISCUSSION QUESTIONS

1. What are some facts about time that we need to remember in order to understand how to manage it?

2. List some causes of time problems. Suggest ways to overcome each one.

3. Discuss specific ways to make better use of the time we have.

4. Keep a time record log for a day. Do it again after you've had a chance to apply some of the things discussed here. Evaluate your progress.

5. What can we learn by looking at the new generation and its use of time?

Chapter eleven

Training and Development

Sooner or later, good supervision must be measured by what employees are doing, not by what the supervisors do. They won't be able to do the job unless they've been trained, and they won't be trained unless the supervisors train them or make arrangements to get it done. Training is more than just showing or telling people how to do things, what not to do to prevent accidents, and how to protect equipment. There are some specific ways to handle training, and all the evidence indicates that some kinds of training are better than others, and that we can tell good training from bad just by watching how it is done. We should follow specific, time-tested steps to assure ourselves that we've done the job correctly. If we don't follow these steps, we can have no confidence that the end results will be satisfactory, even though we've put in the time and the employees *feel like* they've been trained!

Positive supervision assumes that people can and want to learn and that we can teach them. If we approach the training in just that mood, we can be certain that the end product will be a better-trained employee. Going into a training session feeling that it is a waste of time will most likely *make it a waste of time.* Training can never be viewed as something that takes time away from either the supervisor's or the worker's job; rather, it must be considered a contribution to the time-saving effort and certainly a regular part of the job. In this chapter we need to look at the steps as well as the attitudes needed to make training successful. The newer workers aren't about to stand still and wait for ten or fifteen years to learn how to do their jobs, as many of the older supervisors did when they first came to work. No amount of logic will explain to them why they should be given a job to do but not be trained how to do it. To make it even worse, they will surely not stand still while we appraise them as not having done the job properly when we have failed to give them adequate training. None of this is necessary, though, for we can do a good job of training. Let's see how.

KNOW THE JOB

In Chapter 7 we talked about the importance of making sure we know exactly what we want the employee to do before we think of discipline. The same is true for training; we must know exactly what we expect of the employee before we start the training. An oft-quoted saying is, "If we don't know where we're going, we may end up somewhere else." In training, we call this setting standards for the job. Briefly, it's just a way of saying that if the employee were doing the job the way we wanted it done, what would he or she be doing? This doesn't mean the above average employee who always does everything better than anybody else; it means knowing just how we want the job done by *anybody* who is in the job. This standard must be both realistic and measurable. It can't be a dream of someday

"Of course, you'll get a little training on how to operate it."

213

hiring an employee who will be able to do a perfect job; it must be a standard that we can expect from the typical employee, *with the proper training.* The standard should also be realistic for the existing job conditions, not something that design engineers have done in the laboratory or in a make-believe work place. To put together a set of standards for each job, we must consider the noise, the interference, the working conditions, the supply of raw materials, and the work flow. If we do it well, we might even avoid some training, because the employees on the various jobs simply look at the standard and see from it what is expected of them. Rarely, though, can we limit our efforts to this, and training is the logical next step.

PREPARE FOR THE TRAINING

Setting standards might be considered part of the preparation; however, because we actually do it before we even hire employees, it precedes the training preparation. If we get ready to do the training and discover that we really don't have any standards, then by all means setting them is part of getting ready for training. As we think about training, we must prepare both ourselves and the employees who are to be trained. We prepare ourselves by preparing our minds to the point where we are excited about being able to help our employees do something they can't now do. We are enthusiastic about teaching them something, and we are excited about training because it is a part of our job and something about which we should be informed because *it is* a part of our job standard. We also prepare ourselves by reviewing both the standards and the procedures for on-the-job training. We review the job, making certain that we know each of the steps, the reasons for the steps, the safety standards, and the particular areas that are difficult to learn or to perform correctly.

Once we've determined that we know all the necessary details about the job, we think about preparing the employees. They need to know that there is a good reason for the training and that there are some areas of the job that they can't do as well as they should in order to meet the job standards. Training is not punishment, but rather a good opportunity for them to learn to do their job properly. They need to see that they are being held accountable for the *whole* job and that they are being trained so that they will do well on the appraisal, get the job done, and be prepared to move on to another job later. Of course, everything we tell them about training should be positive; no threats should even be implied. We also need to make it very clear to the employees that training is as much a part of their job as doing the work. The fact that we're taking time away from their work schedule shows that training is important and not just nonproductive time.

Another positive aspect of our preparation with the employees is to assure them that they *can* learn what we will train them for. They must see that the job standard is possible for *them* to achieve and that they can do so through the training. The fact that they are not doing the job properly now doesn't imply that they are poor employees or that we're dissatisfied with them. The truth is, we are training them because they have progressed to the point where we think they are ready to do more than they're doing. It's a compliment, not an insult, to them that they are going to be trained.

The final preparation we need to make for training are preparing the training place, choosing the time, and gathering the materials. We should pick a place where there are as few distractions as possible and schedule training for a time when there will be fewer people than normal. We should pick a time when the employees aren't busy or aren't preparing to go home or just coming on the job and thinking about things to be done. This doesn't mean that we can't train at the beginning or at the end of a work period, but we should pick times when the employees are not thinking about urgent things that will cause them to want to get the training over. Some days are better than others and some times are better than others; we need to pick these based on the things we've been talking about. If the training requires equipment, tools, forms, or copies of work material, we should have them handy. The training should resemble the job as much as possible. The training environment should look like the job, sound like the job, smell like the job, and in every way *be* the job or as close to it as we can get. Ideally, it will actually be the job, using the same materials, tools, and equipment that are used right on the job. It should also be the same work, and it can even be a part of the actual work. We need as much realism as we can get, and there's no better place to get it than right on the job.

FOLLOW PROPER TRAINING STEPS

We mentioned that there are some specific steps to follow in training. If nothing else is done right, this certainly should be the thing to concentrate on most. First, let's look at some basic facts about learning. We know that people learn much better if they *see a need for the learning.* We've already talked about taking a positive approach to setting the stage for learning by telling the employees that they are ready for the next stage in their developmental program and need some training for it. They will see that they need the training to be able to do something they can't do now to be successful on the job and to be more valuable to the organization.

Next, we know that people learn much better if they are involved *during the training,* rather than just listening or watching somebody go through the steps. They may think they are following what's happening, and they may even understand it while they look and listen; but after the telling and showing are over, they'll have a hard time doing it themselves.

Next, we know that people *forget pretty rapidly,* and this means that they need to do the operation during the training and on the job as quickly as possible. Training applied immediately after it is received won't be forgotten; if not, it will be forgotten when the time comes to use it. This leads us to something else we know about adult learners that isn't necessarily true about children: Adults live in a "here-and-now" world and will just wait to learn something until they *see an immediate need* to learn it.

Finally, we can be certain that people will learn and remember things *they have done and said,* but not much of what they have heard and seen. There is more involved in this than just getting them interested; it includes working on their minds and their muscles to train each to remember facts and do actions, respectively. Usually, we call this learning "psychomotor" skills; as already stated, there are some specific steps:

Step 1.   **We tell** employees what is to be done, how it is to be done, and, if it's important, why it's done this way.

Step 2.   **We do** the operation step-by-step as we want the employees to do it.

Step 3.   **They tell** us what, how, and why, just as we told them. If they get any part of this step incorrect, they do not go beyond it. If they're wrong, we start over with our part.

Step 4.   **We do** the operation, *if* they've told us everything correctly. We want them to see the operation

done as they've told us, but not if they've told us
incorrectly.

Step 5. **They tell** us again, because we want them to
have it in their minds before we try to get it in their
hands. Again, they must tell us correctly or we go
back to step 1.

Step 6. **They do** the operation, *if* they've told us correctly. Now they are ready to begin the practice.
If they do it incorrectly, we should be able to go
back just one step and have them tell us what to
do, catching their own mistakes.

This system is pretty simple, but it pretty well guarantees
that the employee will remember the right things and be
able to do the job when the training is over. It requires that
we know both the steps in the training and the steps in the
job.

For some reason, supervisors like to let employees
watch while they demonstrate, never letting them get involved until all the talking and doing is over. The employees don't know that this isn't good training, so they watch
and listen the best they can, hoping they are following
everything properly. When through with the training, the
supervisor may say, "Okay, now you try it," without asking
the employees for any explanations. The employees hardly
use their minds or memories at all; even though they may
perform the operation correctly at the time, the next day or
next week they may be doing some of it incorrectly. The
supervisor is surprised and asks, "Don't you remember? I
told you yesterday how to do it." The employee doesn't remember and feels like a failure for not remembering something as simple as what has been said. Both the supervisor
and the trainee may come out of it with very negative feelings, all because the supervisor didn't use the proper
steps in training.

FOLLOW UP ON TRAINING

We've already seen that training is a part of the job, not merely something to do when there's nothing else to do. Because training is important, we shouldn't just do it and hope for the best. We need to follow up on the training we've done to make certain we've accomplished the task of teaching an employee to do a job he or she couldn't do originally. No matter how well we think we handled the training or how well the employee seemed to be doing the job during the training, we still need to check how things are going when the employee uses this new skill in everyday work. We've seen the importance of having a job environment during the training, but no amount of effort will duplicate the *exact* day-to-day working conditions. Even if the training was done at the work site with the actual equipment, forms, or customers, it's different when we aren't there. So we should come back periodically to see how the employee is doing, but not to check up on him or her or to try to catch him or her doing something wrong. We have three purposes in being there: (1) to make sure the job is being done correctly—that's our job all the time; (2) to see whether the employee has run into any problems or needs to ask any questions after getting back into the "real" world; (3) to be in a position to give some positive reinforcement if the employee is doing the job correctly—or even nearly correctly.

If we discover that the employee is doing the job well, we should encourage him or her with positive words. If the employee is doing most of it well, we should reinforce that part and do some retraining, repeating the original steps. If we should find that the employee is completely wrong in doing the job, we can be certain that we handled the training poorly. If the employee did the job right during the training, and if the training followed the steps outlined in this chapter, something is very wrong if the employee is now doing the job completely wrong. Whatever the case, we train if we think it's needed and mark it off as a job well done when we know the employee is performing up to standard. Where do we go from there? We make a mental note that this employee has this one thing under control and is ready for more training in other things, and we look for other employees who may also need training. Somewhere along the line, we probably need to pat ourselves on the back for transforming a less than satisfactory employee into a satisfactory one. We probably ought to review our training efforts to see whether we have the steps down to where we feel comfortable with them and to see where we can improve our efforts. Remember, following the steps is just a part of training. Setting the standard, preparing for training, and preparing the employee for the training are also involved. All these things take time, effort, and skill, and we need to make certain that we are handling them all properly. If so, we are good trainers; if not, we are poor supervisors!

CONCLUSION

In many ways training is a key to success, because it enables employees to do their jobs and because we are satisfactory supervisors when we are able to get the job done by others. They won't be able to do it if they haven't been trained. Since training is a part of our job, we need to think of it as something on which we need to be appraised. If we aren't appraised on it and if we think we're doing a good job, we need to remind *our boss* that we are doing training, which takes time to do well. Otherwise, our appraisal may show that we are taking a lot of time with the other activities of our job in which the training time is counted.

Again, there are some specific steps in training:

We Tell—We Do;
                    They Tell—We Do;
                                        They Tell—They Do;

Then they practice, practice, practice, and we follow up. Not using these proven steps is risking more than it's worth; using them is worth the time it takes, because good training makes good performers.

DISCUSSION QUESTIONS

1. Discuss how good supervision is measured.
2. List ways we can prepare ourselves for training.
3. How do we prepare employees for training?
4. What are the specific steps in training?
5. Discuss the reasons that follow up is so important.

Chapter twelve

Understanding People

So far in this book we haven't used the word "leadership" very much, and there's a good reason. The moment we hear the word we conjure up a mental picture of a person riding the lead horse into battle, with sword drawn and banners flying and the devoted followers—or perhaps just the inspired flock—right behind. This is one kind of leadership that we occasionally see in the everyday business and professional world. Such leaders make a lot of noise, scare a lot of people, inspire a great following, stir up a lot of dust, and often rise rapidly in the organization. Rarely, however, are they successful at training people to do simple tasks like writing better letters, conducting a lengthy meeting, or doing a good job of appraising. The truth is, organizations don't function well because they have such leaders. Rather, success comes from having a large number of capable, not-very-exciting managers and supervisors who know how to handle people well and how to train their employees to get the job done. There isn't a lot of smoke and dust and usually little noise and shouting, but these people and the people who work for them do accomplish a great deal.

"I'm not sure Philby understands leadership as well as he should."

If we expect to be successful in today's work world with the newer employees, we'd better take a long look at our definition of leadership. The days of the boss riding the charger into battle are over for awhile, especially as far as the newer generation is concerned. They won't think favorably about the old autocratic approach that gives them orders in a screaming voice, curses them a few times for good measure, threatens to fire them one or two times a day, and is completely unapproachable. However, they'll have plenty to say and won't mind saying most of it to those who try to get work from them in this manner. In this brief chapter we'll look at a different kind of leadership—one that's much more likely to succeed.

WHAT IS LEADERSHIP?

We've described one kind of leadership, and it's the one people most often think of when they hear the word. However, there are other equally or more effective kinds, which we will do well to learn if we want to accomplish our job in the best possible way. Remember that the term "leadership" implies some form of *followship*. Many have said that looking at the followship a leader gets determines how good a leader that person is. We also need to look at the *kind* of followship we get and the *reasons* for it. We'll see more about this a bit later, but let's make sure we understand that leadership is simply a means of getting a group of people to move in a certain direction. Good leadership is determined not so much by what the mover does but by what those who are moved do.

As supervisors, when we've made plans to accomplish specific goals, in specific times, with specific people, the measure of how well we have done as leaders is how close we get to the goals in the time allowed with the employees given to us. Frequently we hear the phrase "styles of leadership," and it's a legitimate expression; however, it may not say just what we intend for it to mean. If we mean that we can always classify people into certain kinds of styles, we are missing the mark. Some are obvious, of course. We can spot the dictator—the autocratic supervisor who makes all the decisions and tells everybody when to jump, how high to jump, and when to come down. We can also tell the meek, scared-of-the-shadow supervisor, the one who never tells anybody to do anything and whose subordinates either don't do anything or do whatever they want. (While it sounds like this isn't a style at all, it fits our definition of leadership: somebody trying to reach a goal within a certain period with certain people. If the goals aren't met, then it's *poor* leadership instead of *no* leadership.)

The supervisory style that causes employees to be committed to the job rather than to the boss is a style that we can't detect so readily. Even though the boss is almost invisible, everyone is aware of the goals and works well toward them with very little direction. The leadership is there, even though we don't see it. If we examine the situation closely, we'll see that the supervisor has done an excellent job of making certain the goals were met in the time allotted and with the people allowed. Though it's not very apparent, there is leadership present even though there isn't much dust being stirred up and the people probably work harder when the boss isn't around.

BELIEVE IN WHAT?

One way to motivate people is to get them to believe in us as their boss. They, like us, believe we will take care of them and respect our knowledge of the job. They like it when we stand up for them in front of others, and they feel they can bring their problems to us and get a sympathetic hearing, know that we won't be too hard on them if they make some mistakes, and conceive of us as being on their side and their defender in whatever situations they find themselves. Many *successful* supervisors work in just that fashion. Is there anything wrong with this approach if we can get the job done? Of course, there are some cautions. Since they believe in us and get the job done more for us than for the organization, a problem may arise when we're not there. Often they can't function on their own without someone to do battle for them with top management, especially when a problem arises. Since we have been the go-betweens all the time, they may not be able to handle the situation if we are gone and they have to answer to higher management regarding something to do with the job. Even if they give an answer like, "I don't know; you'll have to wait until my supervisor gets back," it's a bad situation for the organization. The job suffers until we get back, so we don't dare leave very often; it would be a major disaster if we were transferred to another job. Things would come to a near halt until a replacemeent was announced, and rarely would the employees be satisfied with the replacement. "Nobody can take the place of *this* supervisor!" they would say; indeed, that would pretty much be the case. It would take a long time for the new supervisor to get the employees back to the level of believing in him or her; until that happened, the job would suffer.

The other approach (and many successful supervisors also take it) is for the employees to *believe in the job* rather than in the boss. This isn't so spectacular, and certainly not as ego-building, but it can be even more rewarding than believing in the boss. If we can get our rewards from seeing the employees performing their job as the organization wants them to, then this way is full of rewards. While this kind of boss will defend the employees, this isn't the measure of the person as far as the employees are concerned. They would rather see the supervisor defend the job than them as individuals. They like to see the job done without interference; if they think they know what they're doing, they like best for the supervisor to keep the higher management people off their backs while they do what they think is important. They are committed to the job, not just to some idea of their own, and they are usually a part to any changes if their supervisors have asked them for suggestions when the job isn't going well.

When bosses such as these described are transferred, there isn't much panic. The job goes on just as it did when the boss had to be away, out of the office, or in a meeting. The workers handled whatever problems arose, and they were quite willing and able to talk to higher management, or anyone else, about any questions or aspects of the job. Their only concern about a replacement is whether they'll be left alone to do their jobs. They will accept anyone who comes along if he or she gives them the same treatment they've been used to and allows them to do their work as they know how to do it.

BUILDING A TEAM

We've seen two extremes in supervision, both of which work. It takes a different approach for each to work, and each has advantages and disadvantages. Both have one thing in common, which is why they both work: they depend on a team to do the job. Even though one group believes in the boss and the other believes in the job, both get the job done as a group. In one case, anyone not doing the job is believed to be hurting things for the boss, and the team doesn't like that. In the other case, a poor performer is seen as someone hurting the job, and hence the group suffers because they want the job to be done correctly. It's called "team building," and it's what ultimately gets the job done as it should be done in the time allowed for it. Both kinds of supervisors will be able to build a team. Each will find that there is little in-fighting or internal guerilla warfare, as it's often called. People aren't looking for someone to blame, and they don't have to try to get out of mistakes they make because they know that, if the job can still be accomplished, the end result will be all that matters. When a problem arises, others step in to help instead of trying to make excuses why they can't. There is no game-playing and underhandedness. The boss doesn't play favorites, and the employees don't tell tales to the boss either to get somebody in trouble or to make themselves look good. When a decision is made, it's made for the good of the organization, not to protect the individual who makes the decision. People are willing to take risks because taking risks is a sign of confidence. While the people are accountable for their failures, they are recognized for their successes, and since they are allowed to make decisions based on their knowledge of the job, they are willing to take calculated chances. They know the consequences and know that the rewards of success are worth the risk of failure. If they fail, they are accountable only to the extent that they can't prevent the failure from occurring again and used bad judgment in making the decisions that led to the mistakes and failures.

BUILDING A STRONG TEAM

The obvious question at this point is, "How do I build such a team? Everybody wants one like it, but where do they come from?" They obviously aren't for sale on the open market, and there is no secret place where they can be bought on the black market. Such teams are built over time, and the younger employees will supply as good material for such a team as the older ones if we learn how to use their talents. We've already seen that they have the capability to work alone and to take responsibility, both of which are ingredients of good team building. Working alone is necessary for the confidence not to depend on others to get the individual job done and to take responsibility. Good supervision will mold this into the team by expanding the responsibility to the whole group instead of giving it to just one person. As supervisors we don't just tell individuals, "This is your responsibility"; rather, we tell the *group* that what comes from them is *their* responsibility and that we have confidence that they will make things come out right.

We've mentioned the word "trust" before, and this is a good place to mention it again. Perhaps nothing is more difficult to deal with than people's trust. When they say they trust us to do the job right, we find ourselves under severe strain to *do it right.* Sometimes we would almost wish they didn't trust us so we wouldn't be under such an obligation; however, it is a good way to build a team whose members will reinforce each other, because trust is contagious. We don't have to make a big scene about it; we don't have to have pages of documents or offer a great deal of praise when they satisfy the trust we've placed in them. We simply let them know that we're behind them and that we know the job will come out right because they want it to. Occasionally we can express this trust to the higher management people when our people can hear us so they know that we're on record as trusting them. This deepens the obligation we've put them under, and they'll worry about it but at the same time appreciate it. Word will spread among the others in the work group, and sooner or later we'll begin to see the signs of a team effort building. Of course, we have to mean it, and we must be willing to allow them to do some things on their own, perhaps without watching them too closely once we know they're capable of making good decisions.

JOB—SKILL MATCHING

One of the skills of a leader is to encourage people to do what they do best. This is just a way of saying we match the people's skills with the job we want done. Nothing is more frustrating than holding a job for which one feels one has no aptitude and no chance of getting off that job. On the other hand, few things are more satisfying than to find oneself doing something at which one feels competent, knowing that it is possible to do what one has been asked to do. A good leader will find out what people do well and see that they have a chance to do that more than anything else. Even if we want them to develop new skills, we don't just throw aside what they do well until they learn a different skill. Job rotation is fine if we want many people who can do many things; if we want to get the job done, however, a large part of the work force must spend most of their time doing what they do well. The rule is never to allow the job to suffer because we're developing people to be better able to serve the job. That's like spending so much time planning that we never have time to carry out the plan.

It takes some finely developed skills to determine just what talents our people have, and part of any leader's job is to develop these skills. It takes more than the ability to appraise people, and it requires that we be willing to give people opportunities to show what they can do. This is somewhat risky on our part, and we must be willing to account for things that go wrong while we're doing this investigation. We also must be able to determine just when people are ready for growth and development, and this means knowing their attitudes and thinking about taking on new assignments and risking some failures. We can most easily make this work by seeing that the employees who are trying out something new also spend a majority of their time still doing things they do well. As they get better at the newer skill, they will be more willing to leave the older ones, and they will eventually get their security from the new one. One of the skills we'll need is the ability to know when the employees are beginning to develop the new skill and when they're beginning to lose their confidence in it. When this happens, we must never leave them alone and let them suffer, but rather do some things with them for awhile and let them know that they have some leeway in going back to the older skill. It isn't permanent, and it needn't be because they will soon be ready to leave this old skill and work on the new one. We can't let people just hop around from one job to another, but we can make room for them to experiment enough to keep from losing their security altogether. Letting people do what they do best for the organization and keeping their confidence up while they are doing it is what leadership is all about.

CONCLUSION

Leadership isn't only a matter of being the first into the battle and the last to retire, even though we are battered and bruised. It's basically a matter of getting a specific job done with specific people in a specific time. It sounds easy, but it isn't; no one has said it is. It must produce a team, and to this extent the leader is like the person on the horse against the enemy—there must be somebody following in order to get the battle won. The battle isn't on the battlefield where the cannons are roaring, but in the day-to-day routines that are carried out by people who believe enough in the boss and in the organization and in the job itself to do whatever it takes to get it done. Some may call it loyalty, and in a way it is. But it's more than just a matter of saying to themselves, "I can do something well, and the organization knows it well enough to let me do it. There are a number of people in the work group who are just like me, and together we form a team that can get the job done whether the boss is present or not. The supervisor knows I'm not perfect, tells me my weaknesses and my strengths, and allows me to do enough on my own to develop both my skills and my confidence. I can't do everything, but I have the confidence that I can learn other things to do." All this put together makes the supervisor a leader who is practicing the best kind of leadership, even though its rewards don't include many medals or marching bands along the way. Even our people may not realize how good a job of supervision we're doing, but we'll know we're getting the job done. If we're the right kind of leaders, we'll let the people under us get the credit anyway, and we'll get pleasure out of knowing that we took the people, the raw materials, the time allotments, and the goals and put them all together to get the job done. If we do that consistently enough, there'll be a few medals for us!

DISCUSSION QUESTIONS

1. What is leadership and how is good leadership determined?

2. What are some different kinds of leaders? What can be said for each type?

3. Contrast motivating by getting our people to believe in us versus by getting them to believe in the job. What are the end results of each of these methods?

4. Discuss the importance of "team building." How can we build a strong team?

5. What is involved in job–skill matching?

Chapter thirteen

Developing a Positive Mental Attitude

Throughout this book we've talked about the importance of keeping a positive attitude. Considering all that supervisors face during their days at work, to suggest that this is easy is to ignore reality. Often it must be done in the face of entire organizations that are very negatively oriented and full of "Thou shalt nots" in their every order, sign, and written policy. Further, the positive attitude must be created and nurtured in an environment that is often hostile to people because of many who believe that people are just basically no good. The newspapers are full of stories about little old ladies who have been attacked while everybody stood around and laughed, or about children who were mistreated or neglected by their unloving parents. Today's media and books and many of the things we see day in and day out tell us that it's a very negative world. If we allow ourselves to believe all these things, we'll find that it is indeed very negative. But there is another side to which we must direct ourselves: that "brighter side of life," which says that there is good in everybody, that people are basically good, and that we can improve our opinion of them if we just try to understand them a little better. If we can teach ourselves to start out by believing that there is some good intent in what people do and say, we'll be more likely to find the good in them than if we start off by assuming that they mean to do us harm and that they're up to no good.

None of this is meaningful, though, unless we *start with ourselves.* We must learn to like ourselves, to believe in ourselves, to know ourselves well enough to know that we do have good intentions, and to believe *that we are all right.* We must work to develop a positive mental attitude (PMA) with which we approach every situation. With PMA we tell the people what they've done well, not just what they've failed to do. We look at their work and see how close they are to the finish, not how much they still have to do. We look at the younger workers and decide that they have a lot going for them and can do much to improve things around the work place. These are all positive motions. They come from a mental position that is positive and can't be faked for very long; they certainly won't come from a self-denigrating position. If we don't have a positive self-image, we can't sustain a positive mental attitude for very long. If we get down on ourselves, it won't be long until we're getting down on others. In this chapter we'll see how we can improve our self-image, and hence how we can get the beginnings of a PMA.

EMPLOYEES REFLECT US

All supervisors want their employees to have positive attitudes and abhor situations in which they answer negatively. If we tell our people to do something, we don't want them to shrug their shoulders, frown, mumble something under their breath, or stalk off sullenly. That's a bad world in which to exist, especially when it represents the people we are expecting to do the work. These are our people, and they have a negative attitude. How did it happen? What can we do to change it? Is it our fault? It would be too much of an oversimplification and a generalization if we were to say that our people simply reflect their supervision; yet, in a real sense, this is a fact. If we approach every situation with a sour look and negative word, it shouldn't surprise us if our people begin to act the same. If we always complain about the way the organization imposes on us, takes advantage of its employees, and never does anything that makes any sense at all, we shouldn't expect our workers to have a bright, cheerful attitude about the organization. On the other hand, if we can come on pretty strong about the organization knowing what it's doing, see the bright spots among all the red tape, and be willing to sit down every once in awhile to explain why the organization does what it does, we can expect our people to be much more sympathetic toward the things that happen. There's no doubt that in many ways they will reflect our viewpoints, and there's little chance that they will have a better viewpoint than do we, however good or bad ours is.

One problem is that we sometimes "inherit" negative employees, and it would be wrong to say that all we have to do to turn them around is show a positive attitude. That's why we can't generalize about the subject. We do know that they aren't likely to get any better if we have the same attitude that they have, and that they might be somewhat better in the long run if they see that we have a positive attitude. Even if they come to us with chips on their shoulders or with bad attitudes toward the organization, the supervision, or the other workers, we do not have the right to respond in like manner. There's pretty good evidence that if we're ever going to get them to improve, we're going to have to do it through a method of "modeling," in which we *demonstrate* the proper attitude we want from them. Parents recognize the wisdom of teaching by example and the folly of telling their children, "Do as I say, not as I do." It doesn't work with children, and it doesn't work with employees.

LOOKING INWARD—A CLOUDY PICTURE

People sometimes say to us, "I can read you like a book," and sometimes they can; however, we rarely, if ever, hear anyone say, "I can read *myself* like a book!" If we ever do hear it, we can be sure that the speaker is either very, very rare or else operating under a very strong delusion. Not many of us see a very clear picture when we look inward. Often those who think they do find themselves sadly mistaken when they see the real truth. Knowing oneself shouldn't be confused with setting goals or "knowing where one's going" as the result of planning, thinking, and trying to put things into place. Rather, it is being able to know just how one feels about things, how one affects others, and how one comes across to them. We've all heard people say, "I'm never like that," when we know that they are *exactly like that,* however "that" is.

We're really talking about *introspection,* and no eye specialists can give us the proper prescription for a clear look into ourselves. Although books have been written on the subject and psychologists and pseudopsychologists have lectured on it, "know thyself" is a difficult command to administer. In the face of all these things, it would be vain and foolish for us to attempt to show how it is done in one chapter. What we can do, though, is to examine some

"These supervisory books are fine, but it's my boss who really needs them."

symptoms that may reveal some things about our inner selves. In this chapter, we're not interested in knowing the whole inner person, but in knowing something about our positive or negative attitude. If we can find some things we do consistently that indicate our attitude, then we can know whether we're operating from a positive or negative viewpoint, even if we can't see inside ourselves very well.

NEW GENERATION—NEW ATTITUDES

We started by trying to decide how we can deal with the younger workers and how we can make them useful, productive workers in the work force that is supervised by those who have quite different attitudes. If we were to ask them what *our* attitudes are, we might not like what we hear. They would probably tell us that we have negative attitudes about everything. They think they have positive attitudes, and for the most part they do. Their attitude is positive in that they feel they can get things done if they try. We feel that things can't get done because we've already tried, but to them that's the definition of positive and negative attitudes. When they hear us say that there's no use in trying to do something differently because we've always done it this way, they shrug their shoulders, mumble and walk away sullenly—and that's what we called negative a few minutes ago! It really was simply a reaction to what they see as a negative attitude in us. Who's right? There is no right or wrong in these kinds of cases, and we aren't trying to prove anything. We can say that our attitude isn't negative but just realistic and that when they get a little more experience, they'll see that we're correct.

What we're really misunderstanding is that this generation has some good thoughts, ideas, and suggestions that come from very positive attitudes—*until we make them negative.* We'd do well to listen to them once in awhile. Many of these younger people operate on a rather quick fuse when it comes to feelings. They haven't been crossed too many times and haven't been told that they can't do things, so they haven't built much of a system for handling it. We talked about that earlier. For now, let's understand that if we consistently turn them down or refuse to listen to their ideas, we will encourage them to develop negative attitudes. It may be that those who seem to have negative attitudes once offered some constructive ideas, only to be told that they weren't being paid to think, only to work. It doesn't take much of this kind of talk to turn people into workers who appear (and perhaps think) very negatively.

SIGNS OF OUR ATTITUDES

As mentioned, some symptoms will give us an idea of what we are really like most of the time. The most accurate predicters are things we do without thinking—our immediate reactions. We can also get another accurate picture of ourselves by envisioning how we act in various situations. For example:

1. You are crossed or somebody disagrees with you. Do you:

Become defensive and argumentative? Is your first reaction to feel the need to prove your point and strike down the person who has dared to get in your way?

Feel rejected? Do you decide that nobody likes you anyway and that they're just looking for a reason to do the job some other way because they don't like you?

Become angry and strike back without much reason? Do you feel that people are just obstinate and unwilling to listen to good sense?

Lose interest in the project or activity altogether? Do you feel that if nobody believes in the work you've done or the suggestions you've made, you'll just forget it too?

Listen to their reasons for disagreement and see if they have a point? Are you willing to change if the other person does, indeed, have a valid argument?

The last example is the positive approach; even though it's pretty obvious, it isn't the way we react all the time. The other reactions are most likely to come from a less-than-positive self-image.

2.   You're given a tough assignment to deal with somebody, and you know that the situation will get sticky and unpleasant. Do you:

Try to get out of it? Do you begin to find excuses why others would be more suitable to do it?

Think first of losing friends, or ending up with people not liking you?

Think more about the hurt feelings and unpleasantness than the good this will do for the organization?

Replay it over and over in your mind after it is over, worrying about whether you did the right thing?

Approach it as a job that has to be done by somebody? Do you decide that there must be some way for something good to come out of it and be glad that you're doing it rather than somebody with less feeling?

As before, the last one represents the positive attitude; the rest are negative. Admittedly, the others are quite natural, but this only suggests that maybe we are trained and developed to think in negative rather than positive terms.

3. You have a challenge that may stretch your ability or even be beyond your capability. Do you:

Simply refuse to get into such a situation or to consider such a task?

Agree to do it after you've gone on record as saying, "I don't think I can do it, but I'll try it"?

List the obstacles and insist that somebody else tell you to do it after they hear the reasons why it won't work?

Take a martyr's attitude of, "No one else would do it, so I agreed to take the risk"?

Approach it with enough assurance that if it is possible for you to do it, it will be done?

All but the last one will sound familiar if you've listened to briefings or meetings where people are given assignments that they feel might affect their careers. The last one will sound familiar if you spend much time around people who are determined that they won't let their attitudes get in the way of their work.

4. When you think of how others are thinking of you, do you think:

They don't think you can do as well as they can?

They may be laughing at you for even being on the job?

"Everybody hates me; I even get the small portions in the cafeteria line"?

They will give you the benefit of the doubt?

How you think others feel about you is one of the most important aspects of developing a positive mental attitude. If you are convinced that others don't like you or don't think you have much ability, you won't think very much of yourself. However, if you give others the benefit of the doubt and know that they mean well and will do well if they can, you'll begin to feel that others think that way about you.

5.   When you think about yourself, do you:

Have fears and doubts and wonder if others will find out about your weaknesses?

Wish you were like others and had their character-istics, looks, charm, or approach to life and work?

Think you could have done better if you'd had the same chances or breaks that others had?

Consider your strengths along with your weak-nesses and decide you haven't done too badly, all things considered?

Some people advocate getting up every morning, looking in the mirror, and telling yourself you're the greatest thing on earth. That's nice; and if you believe it, then it's certainly a positive attitude. The only trouble is that it's not true. *No-body is the greatest.* Everybody has some weakness that others don't have. You are simply what you are, and you can be better than you are but not perfect. You can put some priorities on your weaknesses and try to improve. You can also use your strengths to much advantage if you know what they are and how to use them, but it isn't your role in life to be the greatest. It's not very much fun even to be close to the greatest, because if you are, you have to be on guard all the time to be sure not to make a mistake!

WE ARE WHAT WE ARE

When it comes right down to it, you're an *individual,* nobody else on earth is just like you. You can be better than you are and do more than you do, and you will die with talents you never used. Whatever talents you have and develop are yours; you can choose whether or not to use them, depending on your value system. You can spend a lot of time trying to please others, trying to be what you aren't or trying to change what you are; in the end, however, you'll still be pretty much what you were when you decided to change. This may sound discouraging, but it is simply facing the fact that whatever changing you do will be done *on the mold, not on a new frame.* You will still look a lot like yourself when it's all over; and that's good, because first of all you're the one you have to get along with, and you're also the one you have to like before you can get others to like you!

As you look over the preceding situations you can begin to see if you're positive or negative on the job. If you don't like what you decide you are, it will take quite an effort to change; anytime you think you need to change yourself in some way, you had better face the fact that you've taken on a very difficult task that will take not only concentration but time. You're undertaking a drastic change in your life if you think you can go from being negative to being positive. It would be very *negative* to say that it can't be done, though, so let's see how you can make this change. You aren't trying to make yourself fit into somebody else's mold, and you can decide on your own what you'd like to be and where you'd like to see the changes take place. This will make the job a little easier.

We don't take time here to review each of the situations mentioned earlier, but it would be a good idea to do it someday because it is in these areas that you will have to make your most noticeable changes. As already said, believing others have a high opinion of you is *one* of the most important considerations in developing a positive self image. The *most* important consideration is to have a *very good opinion of yourself.* That's where you start. If you don't have a very good opinion of yourself in the first place, there's no use saying to yourself, "The next time I have something disagreeable to do, I'm going to do thus and so." It might work once or twice if you're concentrating on it, but it won't be the "real" you; and as soon as you forget to watch, you'll be back to your old habits. On the other hand, if you can think more highly of yourself, you can sustain this new behavior.

You should think well of yourself, not because you have developed a great love for yourself, but because you've studied your strengths and weaknesses in light of your job and others around you and have decided that you do have some abilities to do things as well or better than others. When you see weaknesses, you don't get down on yourself; you just decide whether you want to live with them or correct them. If you decide you can do the job just as well with them or that you have some other strengths that will offset the weaknesses, then you go on from there, not with a dejected, rejected outlook, but with a *positive mental attitude* that says you like yourself well enough to go into any situation and handle it well enough to get by, and then some. It will take practice. It will also take some perseverance because some people may try to keep you in a negative frame of mind because they feel uncomfortable around anyone with a positive attitude toward anybody or anything. In the long run, you have the choice of either influencing them or letting them influence you. If you have a PMA, then by all means you should do everything possible to influence them. Who knows, you may start an epidemic!

CONCLUSION

There is much around us that is negative, and in order to conform we may find it easier to be the same way. We may, in fact, be a negative person, but we don't have to be. It is hard to change, but since in this case it depends on no one but us, it is easier. We simply take a look at ourselves and decide if we like what we see; if we don't like it, we must decide if we need to change ourselves or our *opinion* of ourselves. In most cases we can change ourselves if we just change our minds about ourselves. Of course we don't want a false view of what we really are, but we at least need to see the good points we have and learn to exploit them. Once we get a more positive mental attitude about ourselves and the world around us, we'll start seeing some good things in others, including some good things about the organization, about our boss, and even about our workers. We'll start to see some of the good things about the younger employees and find ways they can make a more meaningful contribution to the job. The brightest spot about all of this is that when we do find the good things about the workers and start to use them, all kinds of good things will start to crop up. They'll be more motivated than before, and this will cause them to do more good things and to have better attitudes. This will in turn increase our positive attitudes about them and will begin a slow spiral that certainly won't go out of sight. It will continue to climb, and somewhere down the line we'll see a good team at work and realize that our positive mental attitude went a long way toward putting it together. The changes will have been subtle and we won't be able to trace a clear path from where we were to where we are now, but we'll know that we got there. We'll also know that we got there with the present workers and that we didn't have to fire them all, hire a new breed, or wait until everybody got around to thinking like us. At least a little bit of the mystery will be solved, and we can take the credit for the sleuthing that solved it. There may be no plaques on the wall at Scotland Yard in our honor, but we can rest easier knowing that we've taken the work force that was hired and got the job done. We can't rest on our laurels, but we can pause for a refreshing breath or two. We've earned it!

DISCUSSION QUESTIONS

1. Discuss the importance of a positive self-image in sustaining a positive mental attitude toward others.

2. Does "Do as I say, not as I do" work in our relationships with our employees? Why or why not?

3. How is knowing oneself and setting goals different from knowing where you're going?

4. Why is it so difficult to look inward and get a clear picture of ourselves?

5. We can get a pretty accurate picture of ourselves by envisioning how we act and react in various studies. Test yourself:

   a. You are crossed or somebody disagrees with you. What is your response?

   b. You're given a tough assignment to deal with somebody and you know that the situation will get sticky. What do you do?

   c. You have a challenge that may stretch your ability. How do you deal with it?

   d. What do you think others think of you?

   e. What do you think about yourself?

Chapter fourteen

Supervising Tomorrow

It has been nearly two decades since the first of the "baby boomers" hit the workplace en masse. They have made their mark and left changes in the wake of their almost instantaneous and most spectacular entrance. They have been "cussed and discussed." They have been analyzed and explained. Mostly, they have been integrated into the workforce, but certainly not forgotten. Many are now beginning to move into supervisory ranks, and new problems are arising as a result. So, what happens now? What can we expect the next few years to look like? Is there a return to the "old" values? Is there still an adjustment to be made by them and the rest of the workforce? What will it be like, "Supervising Tomorrow"? We'll see the answers to these questions in this chapter.

TWO DECADES LATER

It's now been a long time since the post-World War II youths came into the job market and spawned such books as this. Those who lived by the motto, "Never trust anyone over 30'' are now 30 years old. To a large extent, they have been absorbed into the workforce, though not without much pain and anguish on their part and the part of those whose lot it was to supervise them. In many situations they *are* the workforce—where older employees have been offered early retirement or have reached retirement age and forced to leave the organization; where the organization has sought to bring in those trained in computer use, who understand "chips" as well as the older generation understood wrenches and screwdrivers. They are a part of whole new industries that weren't even in existence a few years ago.

We've had a good chance to look at them and see them in action as they act and interact with those around them. We've seen them attempt the adjustment into a workforce that was sometimes perceived of as hostile and sometimes was hostile towards them. From what we've seen we can get an idea of what we can expect from them in the future. We've been able to observe their impact on the workplace and the workplace's impact on them. They are no longer outsiders looking in. They are, in many cases, the "in" crowd.

We've seen the sometimes subtle, sometimes not so subtle changes made by old-line supervisors as they have adjusted to this change in the workforce attitude and values. We've seen older supervisors make adjustments in their own personalities and values, not only to accommodate the "new kid on the block" but to enjoy some of the fruits of the new thinking, and we've seen older supervisors examine and become even more convinced that they are "right" in their long-held value systems. We've seen the newer workers change their values also, adjusting to a lifestyle that was not necessarily to their liking but more comfortable to live with than fight against. In all of this, we still find that major differences exist between the generation of the 50s and later, and the generations before that. Major differences exist in basic philosophies in the following areas in particular, and others we'll not discuss:

1. There is still a strong influence of self-centeredness, giving rise to the title, "Me Generation." Because of much self-generated thought and introspection, many decided that they themselves had the answers to most of the world's problems, especially that part of the world that was theirs to live and work in. Rather than describe it as *selfish* it is perhaps better to continue the term self-centered. It is the nature and personality of this particular group to think in terms of what the organization can do for them, rather than what they can do for the organization. Lest we misunderstand, most generations feel that way, but this one is not afraid to express it openly. Other generations thought that if they put the organization first, perhaps it would result in good for themselves.

2. There is also still in evidence the strong need to get and experience things quickly, bringing about the "Now Generation" title. It was not the nature of the upbringing of many of this generation to wait for things they wanted, whether it be a new bicycle or getting out of Viet Nam or cleaning up the streams and air. Their impatience has manifested itself in the workplace, and still does. (We'll see later that this impatience has produced an interesting result where the newer people have moved to supervision!) Just as they don't see a need to wait for personal things, like a new house, new cars, new gadgets for their comfort and enjoyment, they see little need to wait for promotions or for action decisions by management. "I don't care if you did have to do this dumb-dumb job for twelve years before you got promoted, I don't plan to stick around that long if that's what it's going to take to get ahead around here."

3. This group of workers has maintained its high degree of self-confidence and self-reliance. They believe in themselves. They aren't afraid to venture out, take risks, face losses—perhaps because they've always had someone to "bail them out" if they got in over their heads. This self-reliance has made it go well for them in most cases, since they aren't afraid to risk their jobs or careers when offered a challenge. On the other hand, when combined with the impatience they often possess, they are inclined to expect quicker results from management. They then get disgusted with the decision, believing they could have made a better decision in less time. But the self-reliance has given rise to new ideas and new ways of doing things, and certainly has resulted in many useful innovations that probably wouldn't have come about if this group had not come along with their views of how to get things done.

4. Perhaps the thing that has brought about the most consternation is this group's apparent lack of commitment to the job, the boss, or the organization. This has been a constant source of distress among the older supervisors, and continues to be so. In actuality, it may well be that rather than lack of commitment, it is the outspokenness of this group that *sounds like* a lack of commitment. The older employees, especially the supervisors, were in the habit of thinking the things being said, but rarely voicing them— except in the privacy of a carpool or a quiet lunch. There is still ample evidence, though, that the commitment isn't as high, as seen by the frequent job changes and the willingness of the newer employees to admit that they have no intention of staying on a particular job if it doesn't meet their needs soon and often. The idea of hiring only those people who have not changed jobs very often is rapidly becoming a philosophy of the past! This isn't to suggest that "loyalty" should be a requirement for continued employment with an organization. Performance is still the number one criteria for keeping anyone, and will remain that for as long as we have employees.

With all these things still existing, what can we expect for the future? How will all this effect the workplace and the daily lives of those in that workplace? We'll see it as we go further in this chapter.

WHAT KIND OF SUPERVISORS ARE THEY?

As this "new" group of workers ceases to be new anymore, and moves into the supervisory and management ranks, what are we seeing and what can we expect? The entire body of evidence isn't in yet, of course, but we have some indications of what we can expect in the future as this group becomes the "older" supervisors, supervising a new crop of youths. First of all, there has rarely been a dramatic change in these people as they move from worker to boss. There is no sudden loyalty to the organization and to the profit picture and to the customer relations effort. There is a commitment to their immediate job, however. It's probably better to call it a *commitment* than a *loyalty.* They have a pretty strong competitive spirit and like to "win." If they have been assigned a job to do, they want to get that job done. Where older supervisors wanted to win one for the company, this group is more likely to want to win one for themselves, and perhaps for their group.

The organizations have learned to live with this kind of commitment, and management never really cared much about where the loyalty lay, if the job was getting done consistently. With some irony, we note that many of the things that these people didn't like about their older supervisors are showing up in their supervision, though for different reasons. For example, the older supervisors tended to be fairly autocratic, reasoning that the subordinates should be glad just to have a job, so they shouldn't have to be "babied" to get them to perform their jobs. Their idea of good supervisory–subordinate relations was the supervisor giving orders and the subordinates carrying them out without question. There was no room for "Why?" and the newer workforce has driven the older bosses wild with just that question. Now comes the problem: The newest workers are still asking "Why?" The new supervisors don't object to the question and usually don't react as though asking a question is automatic insubordination. However, because they have the impatience of wanting to get things done immediately ("NOW"), they see any question as a roadblock to getting the job performed right now. Hence, their reaction is "Just do it and I'll explain later!" or "Never mind why; just do it!" From all appearances it looks and sounds like the old "autocratic" supervision we found in many older supervisors. The truth is, it *is* autocratic by any definition, but the cause is quite different.

Some had expected a large amount of compassion and understanding to come from this new generation of supervisors, since much of their past was full of such words and accusations against the older management's lack of these things. It was also expected that there would be much understanding of people, their motivations, their moods and their goals. It appears that this isn't going to be the case. What seems to be happening is that these new supervisors look a great deal like their forerunners, in most cases showing a lack of understanding of human nature. They show the same lack of human relations skills as do the older supervisors, and respond to actions with much the same reaction as supervisors have throughout the years. As many suspected would happen, *they are acting just like people!* Their common sense is no better than that of others through the years. They act in ways that "come natural," which is usually wrong, until trained in supervision.

They respond about the same way as others to supervisory training, though seem to accept statistical data from psychological studies more readily than the older supervisors do. They like to see the "systems" aspect to managing people, and make efforts to apply the systems. They have the same reticence in doing things that sound like pampering employees, though they understand the idea of getting employees involved in decision making—as we'll talk about later—more easily than the supervisors of a few years ago. While there is apparently less overall respect for authority or higher management, there is respect for people in general. This respect makes "employee involvement" a more practical and workable activity.

This group of new supervisors have less enchantment with long hours usually associated with supervision, hence find this not to their liking. In some cases we find that they become better delegators, just to avoid the extra work time. Delegation comes hard for most of them, though, since they prefer to depend upon themselves rather than others to get the jobs done. In these cases, they will often just let the work go until the next workshift as opposed to putting in long hours of overtime. Money is a big issue with this group, and the idea of not getting paid overtime for the extra hours isn't very exciting to them. They are more likely to say that better management decisions in the first place would have made the last-minute urgency unnecessary. The job will get done, probably better than the older supervisors would have done it, but on the schedule of the supervisor, not the organization.

EMPLOYEE INVOLVEMENT

One of the biggest problems the new workforce had to adjust to was one of not feeling like a part of the organization. As we mentioned earlier in the book, when they came into the workplace it was the first time in their lives they had been a part of a *minority*. They'd been the majority in every institution and situation they'd associated with up until that time—school, home, community, church, etc. They not only were not a part of a vocal majority, but this was the first time in their lives they had been a part of an institution that did not state serving them as its purpose. The workplace made it clear that the organization was here when they got here, expected to be here when they left, and could probably get along without them. They definitely didn't get any warm feelings of "belongingness."

It was appropriate, if not on purpose, that organizations have become increasingly conscious of the need to get employees involved in some of the key activities in the organization, such as quality control. With the advent of forms of "quality circles," people found themselves being asked by management to help solve problems at the worker level. The newer workforce was definitely ready for such involvement. As supervisors, they can make this kind of system work well. It may be that they will be more involved in employee participation than they will be in the end product of quality, but they will accomplish the same results.

THE COMPUTER AGE

The future of the new workforce is in the already-existing "computer age." While the older supervisors may cringe and leave the computer stuff to the younger folks, the newer supervisors will come in with computers at home, and with *children* who are experts in their uses. We might think of it as a case where the computer will have to wait for the older generation to catch up, and the newer generation will have to wait until the computer technology catches up to them. The newer generation will be looking to the computer to solve their problems, while the older generation will find the computer causing them problems. As we stop here to mention some things about the computer and it's capabilities and limitations, it will help us to understand that much of what we'll be talking about will be perceived as a threat by the supervisors of years gone by, and as things that weren't even needed—much less possible—when they became supervisors.

What Can a Computer Do?

Most people who are coming into the supervisory ranks today recognize that the computer is essentially a piece of equipment that will do only what it has been programmed by humans to do. With the proper programming, it will do quite complex calculations, working with the great quantity of information it has the capacity to store. It can follow instructions and analyze the information in a myriad of ways. It can, of course, display that analysis or other information in many forms, rows, columns, or graphically. Again, it is no better than the programmers, and can do nothing more than what it has been instructed to do. (We'll not go into "artificial intelligence," other than to say that the future will hold computers that can analyze their own functions—as they are instructed to do—and refine the instructions it has been given. That will frighten some of the older supervisors, excite the newer ones!)

Applications for the Supervisors

The newer supervisors will find themselves assisted greatly by the computer and turn to it constantly. Here are some of the uses we'll see—as, indeed, we are already seeing.

Inventory

One of the easiest applications for the supervisor is in the materials-planning and inventory field. With little effort the entire inventory control process can be done by computer, getting the right parts and shipments to the right places, counting stock and giving advance warning of potential shortages.

Operations Activity

Anything that is routine or any information we need when things aren't routine can be obtained from the computer. This means that production control is at the supervisor's fingertips, but so is information on accidents or malfunctions.

Maintenance and Scheduling

The supervisors can input the needs for people and machines to be working for specific purposes at specific times, and can also program the maintenance for slack times.

Personnel Functions

Not only can the laborious tasks of keeping up with all the wage and salary activity be computerized, but any other personnel data can also be stored, retrieved, and analyzed, including appraisal information and education and training records. It also allows for the storing and use of information on employee scheduling, vacation, sick leave and overtime.

Trending and Forecasting

Supervisors have access now to what the future will be, as a result of the computer's ability to take historical information and show the direction the activities being studied are going.

Robotizing

The name is new, but the operation isn't. The idea of a robot is simply having a piece of equipment do an operation as simple as turning a valve or as complex as molding an entire automobile. The computer has made it possible for complex and routine operations to be done entirely by machines (robots), relieving the drudgery and sometimes inconsistency of humans. The new supervisors will see much of this kind of activity. While machines neither come in late nor go on strike, it is still a different world from what the older, people-oriented supervisors are used to. It will be less of a threat to the newer ones.

CROWDING AT THE TOP

One of the most difficult challenges facing the workforce of today, especially the supervisors, is the over-population that exists at their level in the organization. Several things combined to cause "bunching" at their level. The baby boom itself put many more people into the job market at the same time than we had ever had before. The boom in the economy in the 60s got most of these people into the workplace. As long as these people are in the workforce, that crowding will exist. (It will also be a major problem when they retire, because there isn't the population boom behind it, and many of them will retire early.) As they attempt to move up the supervisory ladder, they'll find many others their same age, with similar educations and job experiences, and with equally good references and records. By the time they have reached the age of fifty, at a time when they hope to be moving up into a respected management position, they'll see many more just like themselves looking for the same job.

This will result in several things, and perhaps some we don't know about. Their natural restlessness and impatience will no doubt lead many to seek other jobs and other opportunities. Most likely the opportunities won't be there and the frustrations will continue to exist. Some will resign themselves to their fate of not getting a higher job and will seek fulfillment outside the job. The job will simply be seen as a place to fund the activities that are more important anyway. This roadblock to their careers, together with other things that will engender frustrations in their lives both on and off the job, will cause many to seek to rid themselves of the "establishment" and go for a business of their own. With their usual confidence and willingness to take risks, this is the most obvious choice for many, and a large number are already seeking this route. The amount of success—since management skills and financing are keys to success in individual enterprises—is yet to be determined.

WHERE WILL IT END? (CONCLUSION)

Perhaps we haven't solved the mystery we started in the first chapter. However, we have seen some things that will continue to work, because people are always going to be people, wherever and whoever they are. As we look back over the last couple of decades, we can't help but be impressed with how well the "new generation" has been accepted and absorbed into the workplace. This is a credit to the old-line supervisors, the new work force, and the free enterprise system we operate under. The changes that have been made will be with us for a long time. Just as the generations of the 20s, 30s, and 40s were pretty consistent in their value systems and their actions, the generations that have followed have been and will be consistent in their values. It will take some major eruptions in the life-styles and living conditions to make a drastic change. At present, there don't seem to be any on the horizon.

DISCUSSION QUESTIONS

1. Consider the following "attitude" areas and to the best of your knowledge, compare employees of the different eras as shown:

Attitude	1930s–1940s	1960s–1970s	1980s
Loyalty			
Security			
Money			
Dependence			
Quality			

2. Consider, with examples, the things that made the workplace of today have the value systems they have, and decide what advantages these give them as hourly workers and supervisors today.

3. Allowing for exceptions to all generalities, discuss the major problems we can anticipate with the workforce of the 1970s as they come into the supervisory ranks.

4. Brainstorm some of the technological advances that might come into being in the next ten years that will work for and against the new workforce.

5. Imagine that the year is 2,000. You are writing a book about the make-up of organizations and the type of people at various levels. Describe what it might be like, considering that those born in 1950 will be towards the top of the organization, those born in 1970s will be the first line of supervision and those born in the 1980s will be the new workforce. (Since this is speculation, there are no right answers, so let your imagination go in any direction it wishes!)

Epilogue

So, here we are. You've finished another book, your life hasn't been changed, and you probably still don't know all the things you would like to know about the subject of positive supervision. You found some things to think about, though; and anytime we can come away from an experience having done a little thinking, it is a worthwhile venture. Nowhere have we intended to run down the new workers; we've probably been harder on the workers who have been around for a couple of decades. Those who think the job can't be done with the new workers have too much evidence against them coming from people who are getting the same jobs done very well with just such workers. You just have to work at it a little harder than you might like to. It won't take care of itself, but it'll come out fine if you help it along!

> Like leaves on a tree the race of man is found
> Now green in youth now withering on the ground
> Another race the following spring supplies;
> They fall successive and successive rise.
> So generations in their course decay:
> So flourish these when those are passed away.
>
> Pope

Index